YOUR TOWNS & CITIES IN W

NORTH NORTHUMBERLAND AT WAR 1939-45

YOUR TOWNS & CITIES IN WORLD WAR TWO

NORTH NORTHUMBERLAND AT WAR 1939-45

DR CRAIG ARMSTRONG

Pen & Sword
MILITARY

First published in Great Britain in 2017 by
PEN & SWORD MILITARY
an imprint of
Pen and Sword Books Ltd
47 Church Street
Barnsley
South Yorkshire S70 2AS

ISBN 978 1 47386 742 0

A CIP record for this book is available from the British Library

Printed and bound in England
by CPI Group (UK) Ltd, Croydon, CR0 4YY

Typeset in Times New Roman by Chic Graphics

Pen & Sword Books Ltd incorporates the imprints of
Pen & Sword Archaeology, Atlas, Aviation, Battleground, Discovery,
Family History, History, Maritime, Military, Naval, Politics, Railways,
Select, Social History, Transport, True Crime, Claymore Press,
Frontline Books, Leo Cooper, Praetorian Press, Remember When,
Seaforth Publishing and Wharncliffe.

For a complete list of Pen and Sword titles please contact
Pen and Sword Books Limited
47 Church Street, Barnsley, South Yorkshire, S70 2AS, England
E-mail: enquiries@pen-and-sword.co.uk
Website: www.pen-and-sword.co.uk

Contents

CHAPTER ONE

1939

The Clouds Gather

The days and weeks leading up to the war were a strain on many Northumbrians with the news increasingly grim and many coming to the belief that another war was now all but inevitable. Despite this the everyday life of Northumbrians went on, with the weekend before the declaration of war seeing a slew of agricultural and horticultural shows, while weddings and family celebrations went ahead with perhaps renewed vigour in the circumstances. At Rothbury, for example, a celebration was held to celebrate the golden wedding anniversary of Mr and Mrs G. Butters of 17 Woodlands, Rothbury. The couple had recently moved into their new home and Mr Butters continued to work as a sett maker at nearby Ewesley Quarry.

The Butters of Rothbury celebrated their Golden Wedding Anniversary shortly before the start of the war.

Rural communities attempted to maintain a semblance of normality in the build-up to the war by continuing to hold their annual agricultural shows. Just the week before the war began, one of the most popular North Northumberland shows was held. Glendale Show was (and continues to be) extremely popular and a feature in the rural calendar of Northumberland. Held at Wooler, the show attracted a crowd of thousands and was described as, in the circumstances, 'a distinct triumph'.[1] All classes were described as being of a very high quality with the best sheep and horses from both sides of the border being on display. Highlighting the situation, however, was the presence of a stand representing the Women's Land Army which was offering advice and actively recruiting under the leadership of Mrs J.G.G. Rea of Berrington. One of the most prolific winners in the sheep classes was well-known Northumbrian farmer Mr C.I.C. Bosanquet of Rock who won several prizes including the championship cup and the silver medal presented on behalf of the Society of Border Leicester Sheep Breeders; the small village of Rock was exceptionally successful with several farmers from the area winning prizes. Others who were successful included Mr E. Cuthbert, Jun. of Brinkburn New Houses in Coquetdale. The horticultural and industrial classes were also a success as was the extensive equestrian and sporting programme. Notable visitors to the show included Sir Cuthbert Headlam (who was prospective Conservative candidate for Berwick), Captain the Hon.

Recipients of long service certificates at the Glendale show.

Glendale show, 1939.

Claud Lambton, Major J.G.G. Rea, Captain A.L. Goodson, and notable blackface sheep breeder Mr Arthur Cayley of Carham.

Across the north of the county various leek shows, produce shows, whist drives and dances were taking place with attendances being maintained and people anxious to maintain as normal a life as possible. In Rothbury the second annual show of the Rothbury British Legion Horticultural Society was held at Grieves Hall. Once again there was a good attendance and the displays were of a high quality. The show was opened by Lord and Lady Armstrong (introduced by Dr Reginald Armstrong). The most outstanding display of the show was Mr J. Atkin of Harle's open border flowers, including a beautiful display of gladioli. The vegetable classes were also very fine. Elsewhere, garden fetes were held in small communities across the area, such as that in aid of the Eglingham and Old

Mrs Brown at the Glendale show with her champion.

Eglingham garden fete.

Bewick Churches which was held, with the permission of Colonel Henry Roland Milvain, in the grounds of Eglingham Hall.

As we have seen, one of the most prominent organisations in rural Northumberland at this time of crisis was the Women's Land Army and across the area local group leaders were being selected; for example, Mrs Weeks of Thirston House was appointed as local recruiting officer for the Felton area and advertised that she was available to give particulars to any interested parties.

As the show described above was taking place at Rothbury, a sad event was happening in the village. A coroner's inquest into the sudden death by arsenic poisoning of Mrs Phyllis Evelyn Bell of Front Street, Rothbury, recorded the 'most extraordinary nature' of the case.[2] It would seem that poor Mrs Bell had for many years been suffering silently of severe neurosis and a variety of other nervous complaints which were resulting in severe headaches and spells of sickness. Despite the pleas of her husband, Mrs Bell had only reluctantly sought the advice of Dr Armstrong who had established that Mrs Bell's health issues were a result of her nervous anxieties. The doctor was also aware that Mrs Bell was in the habit of anonymously writing ludicrous letters to various Rothbury folk and the fact that this had become public knowledge was adding to her anxieties. Mr Bell had returned from work, as a grocer, at around 2 pm and had discovered his wife dead on the floor. Dr Armstrong testified that he had arranged an appointment with a nerve specialist for Mrs Bell but that she had died before this could take place. The post-mortem showed that Mrs Bell had ingested enough arsenic to kill fifteen adults. The police were concerned as they had not been able to trace the source of the arsenic. The coroner, despite evidence pointing to suicide, was unable to reach a firm verdict and could only deliver a verdict on the cause of death as it could not be ascertained whether Mrs Bell had ingested the liquid deliberately or by accident.

Many young men had already had their daily lives interrupted by the approaching war, with Army reservists being called up and civil defence workers being put on alert on 24 August. Large numbers had also volunteered for the armed forces. Amongst these was Sir Hugh Seely, former Guards officer and MP for Berwick, who in August 1939 was the commanding officer of an Auxiliary Air Force squadron.[3]

There had been an early indication of the dangers of the increasingly crowded airspace over Northumberland when two RAF aircraft were involved in a mid-air collision near Beal on 17 August. One of the crewmen, Corporal John Prudhoe, had been killed when his parachute failed to open and the subsequent inquest was held at Amble on 28 August. The inquest heard that four Fairey Seals from No. 2 Air Observers School (AOS) based at nearby RAF Acklington were practicing formation flying when the collision occurred.[4] The two aircraft, piloted by Flight Lieutenant James Mail Bodman and Pilot Officer Patrick Chaloner Lindsey, crashed in flames near Beal and the formation leader, Squadron Leader Horace J.L. Hawkins (accompanied by Dr Laurence Vincent McNabb of Amble (medical officer for RAF Acklington)) decided to land nearby to render assistance but unfortunately his aircraft struck an obstacle and was itself wrecked (though thankfully with no casualties).[5] The inquest had no hesitation in declaring that Corporal Prudhoe had lost his life from multiple injuries after his parachute failed to open (in the opinion of Squadron Leader Hawkins because he had been too low when he left the aircraft) and put on record their recognition of the skill and courage shown by

A Fairey Seal of the type which crashed at Beal.

Pilot Officer Lindsey in managing to crash-land his aircraft 'in a way which had not only saved his own life, but the life of his observer'.

As it became ever more clear that war with Germany was all but inevitable, many adverts in local newspapers anticipated the shortages and thriftiness that had characterised the home front in the last war. Motorists, for example, were urged to save petrol and to ensure that their cars were adequately maintained to ensure that they were not wasting this precious commodity. Adverts such as these, however, were juxtaposed with those which encouraged people, despite the worsening political situation, to buy a new car.

There was some anxiety over the availability and price of foodstuffs in the event of war (especially amongst those who had gone through the First World War) but at Alnwick it was reported that provisions were freely available at reasonable prices (see table).

Item	Price (average)
Eggs (per dozen)	1s 10d
Butter (per lb)	1s 3d
Flour (per stone)	1s 10d
Potatoes (per stone)	1s 3d

Although many could see that war was fast approaching, the government was anxious to reassure the public that war was not inevitable while at the same time making preparations for the evacuation of children and the elderly and infirm. Thus on 24 August teachers in evacuation areas, including large tracts of Northumberland and Tyneside, were notified during a broadcast on behalf of the Ministry of Health that they should, if possible, return to their districts immediately in order to prepare for evacuation. While this was not a definite instruction and the broadcast continued with the vacillating that had characterised government preparations, it did give a clear indication to those who were anxiously following the news. Many schools in evacuation areas were recalled shortly before the end of August to take part in practice evacuation procedures.

Motorists were urged to save petrol through good maintenance and thrift.

The government announced that evacuation would begin on Friday, 1 September, but, continuing with the vacillation, added that 'No one should conclude that war is now inevitable.'[6] The process was expected to take several days and the hope was expressed that it would take place smoothly. Practices had taken place, although there was still little organisation in some of the reception areas in Northumberland.

Alnwick was one of the reception areas for evacuees and was scheduled to receive and house some 1,000 people (mainly from areas of Tyneside). The first 500, consisting of schoolchildren, teachers and volunteer helpers, was due to arrive by train at Alnwick station on 1 September at 1.32 pm with a further 500, consisting of mothers with children under school age, following at the same time the next day.

It seems that Alnwick had at least carried out some methodical preparation for the influx, as the station was serving as a makeshift assembly centre. Well before the arrival of the train carrying evacuees, emergency rations had been deposited at the station along with trestle tables. Volunteers had been on duty well before the appointed time to sort the rations and erect the tables. Once disembarked the children would be organised into groups by the teachers and helpers and would take their forty-eight hours of emergency rations from their allocated tables. The emergency rations were separated into adults' and children's portions. An adult's contained two tins of preserved meat, two tins of preserved milk, 1 lb of biscuits, and ¼ lb of chocolate. Children's carrier bags contained the same rations except they only received the one tin of preserved meat. Once they had collected their rations the groups would move towards the station's exit where they would be inspected by Dr Trevor-Roper, the Medical Officer for Health, and any cases of illness were treated by a first aid party led by Mrs Collingwood Thorp which had set up its base in the general waiting room; the majority of the wartime efforts on the home front depended upon the actions of volunteers such as Mrs Thorp and her party. After leaving the station the evacuees would be escorted to the Northumberland Hall where light refreshments were available. From the Northumberland Hall the plan was for the evacuees to be sent to their billets as soon as possible. Alnwick had been split into twenty districts for the purposes of allocating evacuees (see table).

Dist. No.	Location
1	St. Thomas' Close
2	Clayport Gardens
3	Clive House, Clive Terrace, Grosvenor Terrace, Clayport, Monkhouse Terrace, King Street, Lisburn Street (part)
4	Bailiffgate, Northumberland Street, Barndale House, Council School House
5	Canongate, Walkergate
6	Narrowgate (part), Fenkle Street, Bondgate Within, Market Street, Paikes Street
7	Chapel Lane, St. Michael's Lane, Green Batt
8	Glebe Lands Grey Place, Croft Place, Hotspur Street, Dovecote terrace, Police Houses
9	Bondgate Without
10	Prudhoe Street, Stott Street
11	Percy Street, Howick Street, Lisburn Street
12	Armstrong Place, Beaconsfield Street, Clifton Terrace, Percy Street
13	Hope Terrace, The Dunterns
14	Bridge Street, Duke Street
15	Lovaine Terrace, East and West Parade, Wagon Way Road, Aydon Crescent (part)
16	Aydon Crescent (part), Victoria Terrace, York Crescent
17	Victoria Crescent, St. George's Crescent, Lindisfarne Road
18	Sea View Terrace, Augur Terrace, Greensfield Avenue, Queen Street
19	Alnmouth Road, West Acres, Newcastle Road
20	Swansfield Park Road

Despite governmental assurances, the preparations for war were becoming ever more visible to the people of Northumberland, Air Raid Precautions (ARP) work continuing at a feverish pace. Although recruitment had been in place for some time it had been in fits and starts as the European situation lurched from crisis to apparent stability and back to crisis once more. In Alnwick during the final week of August it was clear that the pace had been increased. The future control office for the district, the council offices, were being sandbagged as was the Fire Brigade control centre at the caretaker's house next to the council offices. Other preparations included the establishment of a first aid post at the Church of England School, where equipment had recently arrived. This was under the command of Dr Trevor-Roper along with Mr R.H.C. Coates and Mrs C. Thorp of the British Red Cross Society (BRCS) detachments. The medical authorities also undertook a final, and rather last-minute, distribution of gas masks at Northumberland Hall.

In addition to the services which would cope in the wake of air raids there were also those civilians who played an active role in the defence of Britain and formed a crucial link in the system of aerial defence which, together with radar, would prove so vital in 1940 and 1941. These were the men and women of the Royal Observer Corps who manned positions scattered far and wide across the county, such as the position just outside Longhorsley. Their duties were to spot and report the numbers and height of enemy aircraft so that RAF Fighter Command could respond in a timely and effective manner.

Charlie Monaghan of the Royal Observer Corps at Longhorsley (from collection of Bill Ricalton).

The scenes were being repeated on the coast at Amble where the local council offices were being fortified in advance of their role as control office, while St. Cuthbert's Hall was being outfitted and equipped as a first aid post and Red Cross Hospital complete with beds and full equipment (naval casualties were quite likely to be landed at Amble). This was overseen by Dr J.A. Longridge and staffed, once more, by local BRCS volunteers.

In both towns, and elsewhere in Northumberland, large numbers of workmen were busy erecting air-raid shelters and digging trenches, the police were now equipped with steel helmets instead of their regular attire and some local activities were being cancelled or curtailed; in Alnwick the Newcastle schoolchildren who had been enjoying their time at the Lord Mayor's Holiday Camp were sent back to Tyneside, many just in time to be evacuated, some to Alnwick.

A People's War?
With war declared and instructions pouring in from the government, local councils were almost overwhelmed by the need for wartime measures such as policing the blackout, providing first aid for anticipated casualties, maintaining the supply of food, and the strains of sustaining a wartime economy. Just the week after the declaration of war Rothbury Rural District Council met to discuss, amongst other matters, the issues of a food control committee and the measures which would be needed to provide for any evacuees.

The evacuation scheme had already resulted in 254 evacuees being housed in the district which had been told to expect, in the first two days, some 1,000 evacuees. However, the government had now put Evacuation Scheme No. 3 into operation and for the Rothbury District this meant that evacuees from Wallsend, Tynemouth, Jarrow, South Shields, Sunderland and Hartlepool would be sent to the area. The council was particularly worried over the estimated 800 evacuees who were expected from Tynemouth and were anxious that many people who had already seen fit to evacuate themselves were offering cash for billets and that this was causing a severe shortage. Members of the council presented evidence that some people were charging up to fifty shillings for rental of a single room. Although the council had asked if any delay in the scheme was possible, the government had, naturally, stated that this would not be possible and that the council should take

Evacuees like these from Newcastle became a common sight in Northumbrian towns and villages.

all measures to ensure that official evacuees were billeted and that, if necessary, the police could be called upon to remove unofficial evacuees from billets. It was pointed out that some people had been enticed by the sums offered by these unofficial evacuees and that those who housed official evacuees made no monetary gain. The response to this was blunt, one member of the council stating simply, 'They must be put out.'

The first of these new evacuees was expected to arrive by train at 10.30 am on Wednesday, 13 September. The evacuees on Wednesday were to consist of unaccompanied schoolchildren while the following day would see the turn of mothers and children, crippled children and blind people.

In order to secure sufficient numbers of billets the local councils also received powers which enabled them to appoint billeting officers whose role it would be to go around the districts to find suitable properties and report back to the authorities. Because a number of residents had already expressed their opposition to this, the councils were also given the power to set up billeting tribunals which would decide on individual cases.

The Food Control Committee was a body which was ostensibly separate from the council but the council appointed its members. The initial composition of the committee consisted of five local traders, two ladies and eight consumers. The traders were: James Oliver of Cowans & Oliver (corn and flour dealers and millers of Thrum Mill, Rothbury); Mr Wilson of Wilson Ninian & Sons (butchers of Townfoot, Rothbury); Mr Blackie (or Balkey) of Longframlington (butcher and farmer); Mr H. Jones of the Co-op; and Mr H. Dixon (Whittingham). The ladies and consumers were: Mrs Snaith of 4 Walby Hill (Rothbury); Mrs Palmer of Harbottle; Mr J. Charleton of Rothbury; Mr J. Snaith of Rothbury; Mr Charles Waddell of Alwinton (farmer); Mr Rogerson of Whittingham (farmer); the Reverend C. Hillis of Elsdon; Mr Cranston George Cowans of Longframlington (farmer); Mr J. Pringle of Netherton South Side (farmer); and Mr James Smith of Ritton White House, Netherwitton (manager of Ewesley Quarry Co Ltd). The local food controller was also the council clerk, Mr W.N. Wade, who had an office in Rothbury from where he undertook his duties.

Many of the evacuees who did find themselves in the Rothbury area found themselves being given a warm welcome and those adults who had accompanied the groups were keen to express their gratitude. In late September a letter from Sister M. Austin (who had accompanied group Tynemouth 6A) was featured in the *Alnwick and County Gazette and Guardian* in which Sister Austin expressed her own feelings. As part of a group accompanying children from a North Shields Catholic school, Sister Austin explained how the children had been given only forty-eight hours' notice to pack and that it was with feelings of despondency that they set off for their destination (which was unknown barring that it was in the Rothbury district) but that the welcome which awaited them at Rothbury Station cheered their spirits. She wished the people of Rothbury well for their charitable welcome and unstinting efforts to find suitable accommodation for the evacuees.

For some evacuees the experience of rural life was eye-opening to say the least. There are common (and true) tales of evacuee children not knowing what a cow or sheep actually was. Others, coming from areas of depredation, were perplexed by the complexities of growing one's own food. One group of evacuees from North Shields found itself in the far north of Northumberland at Milfield being instructed in 'the rudiments of gardening' by the local schoolchildren.[7]

As well as having to cope with an influx of evacuees the local

Evacuees from the cities were instructed in gardening by locals.

authorities in north Northumberland were also confronted with a huge number of often complex problems ranging from civil defence arrangements and the preparation of air-raid shelters to the requirements of central government. As a result, a plethora of committees and sub-committees came into existence in the first weeks and months of the war, usually manned by a combination of local authority members, councillors and volunteers.

Amongst the many emergency committees which were set up in the early days and weeks of the war, one which provoked the most interest and comment was that of the Northumberland War Emergency Agricultural Committee (commonly known as the War Ag). Based in the heart of the county at Bolton Hall, halfway between Alnwick and Whittingham, the War Ag was chaired by Major John George Grey Rea DSO of Berrington House, Ancroft, with the council's side of the work being undertaken by the County Land Agent Mr A.P. Ker who became executive officer to the War Ag. The War Ag chair was the representative of the Minister of Agriculture and was answerable directly to him. The members (who were unpaid volunteers) were assisted by a full-time paid staff which was made up largely of land agents, technical advisers and expert advisers from King's College in Newcastle.[8]

The War Ag had extensive duties which included not only the distribution of good farming practice and advice but also the inspection of farm premises and the establishment of the necessary supplies of labour, machinery and other agricultural supplies. They also advised farmers on what crops to grow and what livestock to rear. Most controversially, they had the power to dispossess farmers who they believed to be incompetent or unwilling to follow the dictates of the War Ag.[9]

Northumberland War Ag Members, 1939	
Name	Place of Residence
Major J.G.G. Rea, DSO (Chairman)	Berrington House, Ancroft, Berwick-upon-Tweed
Mr A.P. Ker (Executive Officer)	Unknown
Mr R. Anderson	Mosswood, Consett, Co. Durham
Mr C.B. Chartres	Mindrum
Rt. Hon. Countess Grey, CBE	Howick
Mr T.W. Haward	Abbey Lands, Alnwick
Mr J.E. Moffett	Peepy Farm, Stocksfield
Mr A.A. Robertson	37 Cliftonville Gardens, Monkseaton
Mr W. Robertson	Stamford

Having learned from the previous war, agriculture was one of the few areas for which adequate wartime planning was already in place and the new Ministry of Food was quickly established. Initially the government demanded that 1,500,000 acres across the nation be put to the plough in order to raise crops and asked the Northumberland War Ag to oversee a county increase of 35,000-40,000 acres. This was part of the two-pronged programme of campaigns to increase home production; the campaign titles became famous as the 'Ploughing Up' campaign and the 'Dig for Victory' campaign.[10]

Being responsible for a very large county, the Northumberland War Ag decided to form a large number of local sub-committees which would be made up of men who knew the local country. These sub-committees were formed using the Rural District Council areas as a basis (the exception being the far south-east of the county which was controlled solely by Tynemouth); in total there were eleven area sub-committees. The make-up of these committees varied but inevitably they contained a mix of experienced local farmers and agricultural experts. This was to ensure that local knowledge was to the fore and that the local farming community would accept the committee members and value their opinions. Their first acts were to publicise the government's £2 per acre subsidy for farmers ploughing up pasture and grassland, to advise farmers that wheat should be planted for the 1940 harvest, and to inform them that the previous restriction on the amount of land that could be used for potatoes had been lifted.

District Sub-Committees (Northern Northumberland), Members, 1939	
Norham & Islandshire **Name Place of Residence**	
Mr J.R. Wood (Chairman)	Castle Heaton, Cornhill-on-Tweed
Mr W.W. Patterson	Ancroft Town Farm, Ancroft, Berwick-upon-Tweed
Mr J.B. Lockie	Ford Westfield Farm, Wooler
Mr J.H. Hedley	Cheswick, Beal
Mr J.D. Davidson	Beal House, Beal
Mr T. Urwin (Secretary)	70 Shieldfield Terrace, Tweedmouth
Glendale **Name**	**Place of Residence**
Captain, the Hon. Claude Lambton (Chairman)	West Newton, Wooler
Captain T.E. Hamilton	Hetton Steads, Lowick

Mr J.W. Sale	Weetwood Hall, Wooler
Mr J.B. Barr	Pressen, Cornhill-on-Tweed
Mr A.L. Goodson	Kilhum, Mindrum
Mr T. Stawart	Lilburn Grange, West Lilburn, Alnwick
Mr W. Smith (Secretary)	Ryebank, Wooler

Belford

Name	Place of Residence
Mr W.N. Villiers (Chairman)	Adderstone Hall, Belford
Mr R. Urwin	Belford Mains, Belford
Mr J. Robinson	Elford, Seahouses
Mr W. Reay	Elwick, Belford
Mr A.R. Little	Mousen, Belford
Mr H. Hunter (Secretary)	Sionside, Belford

Rothbury

Name	Place of Residence
Mr R.D. Scott (Chairman)	Caistron, Thropton
Mr T.O. Donkin	Gallowfield, Thropton
Mr J.O Snaith	Scrainwood, Thropton
Mr J.F.H. Chrisp	Low Trewhitt, Thropton
Mr E.A. Crawford	Cartington, Thropton
Mr J. Elliott (Secretary)	Highfield, Rothbury

Alnwick

Name	Place of Residence
Mr W. MacDonald (Chairman)	Rock Estate Office, Alnwick
Mr M. Malcolm	Park Farm, Alnwick
Mr F. Heath	Chester House, Acklington
Mr J.D. Forsyth	Gloster Hill, Amble
Mr J. Chrisp	Hawkhill, Lesbury
Mr A. Beresford Peirse	Park Cottage, Alnwick
Mr J.M. Frater (Secretary)	Tynely Farm, Chathill

Bellingham	
Name	**Place of Residence**
Mr T.H. Hedley (Chairman)	Garretshields, Otterburn
Mr A.H. Ridley	Park Ends, Simonburn
Mr R. Robson	Hole Farm, Bellingham
Mr S. Dodd	Catcleugh, Otterburn
Mr W.L. Robson	High Chesterhope, West Woodburn
Mr G. Robson	Shieldlaw, Bellingham
Mr E. Thompson (Secretary)	Fellside, Bellingham

Other advice for farmers came from the authorities in control of ARP. Although admitting that farms were usually amongst the safest places to be during bombing, the authorities did give Northumberland farmers some initial advice on actions to be taken in the event of bombs being dropped on their land. In the event of gas attack farmers were advised that byres and other buildings used to house livestock could be rendered reasonably gas-proof by shutting all doors and windows, closing ventilators and by hanging damp sacking over them. To prevent damage from blast bombs farmers were advised to sandbag their buildings to a height of approximately six feet (few did). Acknowledging that enemy bombers could jettison bombs over farmland and with the fear of chemical attack to the fore farmers were advised that any gas bombs dropped should be reported immediately and that animals should be kept away from the area. Furthermore, animals which had been splashed by mustard gas or lewisite should be wiped clean with a rag soaked in paraffin or petrol and bleach applied for five minutes followed by a paste of bleaching powder and water. If the eyes were affected they were to be washed with a bicarbonate of soda solution. All animal feeds which were in the open as well as any open-roofed buildings should be covered by tarpaulins, while stores of grain should be covered with a material which was not easily ignitable. Farmers were also given the advice which applied to other households which was to cover windows with strips of cellulose in order to prevent them shattering.

Once again learning from the previous war, farmers were informed that some soldiers would be made available for harvest labour and that any interested parties should apply to the executive officer at Bolton Hall. It was also hoped that a number of council employees (mainly road workers) would also come forward to act as harvest labourers and farmers would be advised of this (farmers were also asked to give to the executive officer the names of any such men they knew).

Local press reports which covered the formation of the Northumberland War Ag all included an announcement from the War Ag stating that they were sure that the cooperation of farmers would enable them successfully to carry out their duties without having to resort to the 'compulsory powers which they possess'.

Farmers were quickly made aware that they were on the front lines of the war. We have already seen how they were warned of ARP procedures and how War Ags eroded long-held freedoms, but the government was also keen to maintain morale amongst the rural population. The Minister of Agriculture, Reginald Dorman-Smith MP, gave a broadcast on the BBC as early as 4 September which was almost solely aimed at farmers and farm labourers. In the broadcast he stated that the main aim for farmers was to increase production of essential foodstuffs and that for this to happen the ploughing up of ten per cent of arable or idle land would be absolutely vital. Initially this land was to be seeded with wheat or potatoes with the possibility of crops of 'oats, barley, beans, peas, rye, or maize'.[11] Dorman-Smith also urged labourers to stay on the land as their efforts were vital to the war effort. In order to appease farmers and labourers the Minister said that he would ensure that, as farmers were incurring greater costs, it was only fair that they would earn money for it. He added that this would also apply to the farm labourers, and indeed wages did increase in the first months of the war.

One of the issues which confronted local authorities in Northumberland was that of the necessity to instruct volunteer fire fighters, first aiders and ARP workers in the skills which would be necessary in an emergency. Just a week into the war Rothbury Rural District Council heard that one of the councillors, Thomas Carruthers, and two volunteers, Mr Murray Brown and Mr Robert George Bolam (6 Silverton Terrace, Rothbury), had undertaken a fairly extensive firefighting course with Alnwick Urban Council Brigade. The ARP methods of firefighting which had been covered included the use of light and medium trailer pumps, ladder drill, hose drill, sheet jumping drill, classes on hydraulics and water pressure and basic first aid. The three men volunteered to train the nascent Rothbury Brigade which consisted of twenty-eight volunteers and revealed that they were expecting the imminent arrival of a trailer pump for the town.

Minor crimes continued despite the declaration of war and a prime concern in the Rothbury district was the increase in traffic offences. On 4 September Rothbury Court heard a case resulting from a collision between a car and a lorry at Swindon. The 20-year-old driver of the lorry, John Edward Burn of Knowesgate, pleaded not guilty to the charge of dangerous driving and of driving a vehicle with a defective mirror. It seems that the lorry's side window had been smashed and boarded up with wood which meant that the driver could not see the car as he pulled out. The car, driven by Mrs Lorna Kate Dodd, was struck and went out of control for some distance. Mr Burn's employer, John George Forster of The garage, Otterburn, was also charged with having allowed Burn to operate the vehicle knowing that it was unroadworthy. Despite some arguments over the speed which Mrs Dodd was driving both defendants were found guilty with Burn being fined £3 10s with an additional 10s expenses and his employer being fined £2.

An early casualty of the war was the traditional Alwinton Border Shepherds Show which usually took place in October. Due to the war it was announced in late September that the show had been cancelled.

The blackout, as it had been in the First World War, was the source of much grumbling and resulted in a significant rise in the number of accidents. This was hardly surprising given the larger numbers of motor vehicles which were by now in use (though many would be put out of use for the duration of the war due to shortages of petrol). In mid-September a motor-lorry from the Edinburgh firm of J.H. Nicholson went out of control on the Great North Road during blackout conditions resulting in it crashing into a wall and telegraph pole at Broomhouse near Alnwick. Although the vehicle's load of paper was shed into a nearby field, the driver, Mr Donald C. Wood of Edinburgh, escaped serious injury.

The blackout and the availability of air-raid shelters led to an increase in sexual liaisons and consequently a rise in concern amongst the authorities over any perceived decline in moral standards as had

The blackout caused an increase in road accidents like this one at Broomhouse.

been alleged during the First World War. Possibly caught up in the spirit and uncertainty of wartime Britain there were a larger number of marriages than normal during the first months of the war; many of these involved men who were in the services. Just the day after war was declared many of the Northumberland gentry attended the wedding of Mr Peter Roddam Holderness-Roddam of Roddam Hall and the Honourable Moira Massey at St. Michael's at Ingram. On 23 September at Alnwick's St. Mary's Roman Catholic Church, Corporal J. Ronald Thompson of Gateshead married local woman Isabel Marie Coulthard in what was described as 'a very pretty wedding'. Because of shortages of material many wartime brides had to forgo the traditional white gown, with Miss Coulthard being married in a turquoise dress and hat. Sadly, the marriage, like many, did not survive the war; Corporal Thompson, Black Watch (Royal Highlanders, 1st Tyneside Scottish) was killed on 20 May 1940 aged 27.[12]

The same week saw the marriage of Mr Edward Liddell Mackenzie and Miss Violet Gunn at Alnwick's Clayport Presbyterian Church. Both

Alnwick woman Isabel Marie Coulthard married Corporal J. Ronald Thompson on 26 September. Sadly the wedding lasted only months as Corporal Thompson was killed on 20 May 1940.

Edward Liddell Mackenzie and Miss Violet Gunn were both married in their hometown of Alnwick.

The Honourable Moira Massey (pictured) married well-known Northumberland gentleman Mr Peter Roddam Holderness-Roddam of Roddom Hall at the village of Ingram.

The Northumbrian gentry came out in force for the wedding of Peter Roddam Holderness-Roddam of Roddam Hall and the Honourable Moira Massey.

Lance Corporal William Stewart and Miss Annie Arthur were married at Widdrington.

John Slater of Broomhill and Miss Phyllis Ogle of Embleton were married in the bride's home village.

were Alnwick natives and once again the clothing reflected wartime exigencies. The bride received a present of a gold wristlet watch, the bridesmaid a rope of pearls, and the groom a Rolls razor.

Other local marriages to take place around the same time included that of Lance Corporal William Stewart and Miss Annie Arthur at Widdrington Village Church, that of Mr John Slater of Broomhill and Miss Phyllis Ogle of Embleton at Embleton Parish Church, and that of Methodist Minister the Reverend Leonard Knight and Miss Janet Lothian Earle of Alnmouth at Alnmouth Methodist Church.

Boy Scouts and Girl Guides combined their normal activities with

Belford Brownies. Local groups such as these continued their efforts to raise money.

Red Row Leek Club, just one of many which went ahead with their annual show despite the war.

training for activities in the event of a wartime emergency. The Belford Girl Guides, for example, went ahead with their open-air meeting at the end of September. Other clubs also continued with their activities; local leek clubs and allotment clubs were of course increasingly aware that their activities would become more important due to the war.

In the early hours of 14 October the Revenge Class battleship HMS *Royal Oak* was anchored at Scapa Flow. HMS *Royal Oak* had been launched in 1914 and had taken part in the Battle of Jutland two years later. Although attempts to modernise her had been continuous, the battleship was relegated to second-line duties because she was too slow. Scapa Flow was believed to be an impregnable mooring so the watch was minimal and a few minutes before 1 am the *U-47*, which had skilfully infiltrated the harbour, fired three torpedoes at *Royal Oak*, one of which hit. The torpedo struck the bow but damage was slight and many of the crew went back to bed as it was thought that it could have been a minor internal explosion in the ship's kerosene store. *U-47* fired

HMS Royal Oak.

several more torpedoes and a salvo of three struck the battleship amidships at 1.16 am. The explosions ripped through the ship and destroyed the Stokers', Boys' and Marines' messes before causing a complete failure of electrical power. A magazine then ignited and the subsequent explosion caused a fireball which ripped through the ship causing a list of fifteen degrees which quickly steepened to forty-five as the portholes became submerged. The battleship took just thirteen minutes to sink. Of the ship's complement of 1,243 men and boys some 833 were killed. These included over one hundred boy seamen who had not yet reached their eighteenth birthday (the largest such loss in any single action). Included amongst the boy sailors killed was Boy 1st Class John Oswald Harold

Leading Boy Derry who was killed aboard HMS Royal Oak (Berwickshire News).

Derry of Berwick-upon-Tweed. Aged 17, Derry's body was never recovered and he is commemorated on the Portsmouth Naval Memorial and at the wreck of HMS *Royal Oak* which is a registered war grave.

As the first wartime Christmas approached, people were trying to carry on, as far as possible, as normal. Despite this, there were signs of increased militarism and patriotic fervour within society. At Embleton the children of the village, along with the large number of evacuees from the Byker area of Tyneside, were given a Christmas tea party on 21 December. The event, said to be the largest scale in the village's history, was held at the Creighton Memorial Hall and the refreshments were accompanied by a programme of entertainment involving the children, their teachers and some semi-professional performers from the Berwick area. These included Scottish dancer Miss Hilda Fawcus, who also put on a performance as a Shirley Temple impersonator, and tap dancers Miss Betty Bryson and Miss Isobel Evans.

At Branxton there were two separate parties held for the children of the village and twenty-seven evacuees. At the first, held on 20 December, the children were given a fine feast and, although there was no Christmas tree, Santa arrived to give each child a toy; they also received gifts from the host and hostess, Reverend W.N. Clarke and Mrs Clarke. Between the first and second parties a carol service was held on Christmas Eve with the children joining in enthusiastically with the choir. The second party took place on Christmas Day itself when Mr and Mrs John Fairnington treated the little ones to a fine tea, this time with a Christmas tree. The children were playing games and reacted with glee when Santa Claus once again made an appearance.

Lord and Lady Joicey gave a Christmas entertainment and treat to evacuees from Newcastle at their Ford Castle residence. Although many of the children had been given the option of returning home for the holidays some did not want to leave and at least two 'cried so hard when mother came to fetch them that they were eventually allowed to stay "evacuated"'.[13] The presence of evacuees swelled the attendances of many Christmas parties held throughout north Northumberland with small villages rallying round to provide sufficient food and presents. For example the small village of Lesbury had held its annual Sunday School Christmas party on 16 December with local evacuee families being invited to attend. This resulted in over 130 children being entertained with games, presents, a visit from Santa Claus and two toy-laden Christmas trees (donated by the Duke of Northumberland).

In Wooler the church bells rang out at 8 am on Christmas morning and this was followed by a military band which toured every street in the town to play Christmas carols. This was followed by a drum head service held at 10 am in Brewery Park. The service attracted not only members of the military based in and around the town but also a large crowd of citizens. Immediately following the service was a football match which attracted an even larger crowd. Although church services were very well attended, helped by the fact that the weather was described as being more akin to a beautiful spring morning, many locals were involved in the gargantuan efforts to feed the servicemen in the local area. At Glendale Co-operative the list of food served during the day amounted to over 100 turkeys, 40 lbs of pork, 60 large plum puddings, masses of vegetables, fruit, nuts and three large barrels of beer. The meals were prepared by Mr and Mrs David Brown, helped by a staff, and the servicemen were loud in their praise of the efforts made on their behalf. Elsewhere in the town the Picture House screened two showings of a Gracie Fields movie which attracted large numbers, with servicemen being well represented.

In the village of Ford more than 100 soldiers were entertained on Christmas night at the school by Reverend S.C. Bryson and his wife, while on Boxing Day the members of the local Women's Institute hosted a dance for the troops which attracted large numbers of local young folk. This was followed up by a concert on 28 December with a concert party from nearby Spittal.

The men of the 10th Battalion, Northumberland Fusiliers, Home Defence Unit, who were stationed in Berwick, were treated to 'a sumptuous dinner on Christmas Day'. The meal was supplied through the kindness of many friends including Lady Francis Osborne, Miss E. Clay, Lieutenant Houston-Boswell and Major H.R. Smail. The men, all of whom were ex-servicemen, had decorated their quarters with bunting and Christmas decorations and confessed that 'Christmas in khaki was not so bad after all'. On Boxing Day the men of the unit entertained wives and friends, helped by an anonymous donation of seasonal fare; on both days the unit was entertained by Corporal Emery.

For many Northumberland families the highlight of the Christmas period was the fact that many of the young men and women who were serving in the forces were given leave to spend some time with their families over the festive period. With Christmas Day falling on a Monday it was 'a week-end of reunion'.[14] There were several weddings of local service personnel, such as that of Fusilier William Lawrence Hill of Norham. A former pupil at Berwick Grammar School William had gained a reputation as a fine footballer and subsequently played in the Crookham and District League while also serving in the Territorials. Fusilier Hill married Miss Virtue Collis (of Choppington) at Norham Parish Church on 23 December. The bride was described as wearing a maroon dress with gold trimmings and a grey fur fabric coat and, like her chief bridesmaid (her sister), carried a bouquet of chrysanthemums. The best man was Mr John Guthrie and there were four naval men present at the service. Three of these were chief petty officers: A. Hill (the bridegroom's father), James White and Fred Copsey. The fourth naval representative was Able Seaman J. Purves. Also in uniform in the congregation was Sergeant Smith (Berwick) of the Northumberland Fusiliers. After the service a cheerful reception was held at the Victoria Hotel. Other wartime weddings to take place over the festive period included those of Private John Shiel, who was on leave from France,

The local Territorials were called up at the very start of the war (Berwick Advertiser).

of Ancroft and Miss Jeannie Turnbull at Ford, and Private William Welsh and Miss Jean Wood Lough at Berwick Registry Office.

Given that large numbers of north Northumberland men and women were already serving the war effort away from their homes it should come as no surprise that letter writing increased during the holiday season. The employees of the Post Office at Berwick were worked off their feet and an extra twenty-two temporary staff had to be taken on to cope with the rush. The staff worked throughout the night and were thankful for 'the moonlight' which aided them in their deliveries. Throughout the holiday period some 125,000 letters passed through the stamping machine in the town's Post Office (an increase of 15,000 on 1938) with 55,000 letters being dealt with on 22 and 23 December alone. The Post Office still expected a huge rush over the New Year and urged people to post early so as to help the overworked staff.

The people of Berwick made a concerted effort, despite reminders such as the blackout and the presence of many soldiers, to maintain as traditional a Christmas as possible. This was demonstrated by the large crowds of shoppers who thronged the town. The peak of this shopping rush came on Saturday, 23 December, and saw last minute local shoppers rivalled by those who had come in from more rural areas. It was said that 'Thousands flocked to the town during the day and shopkeepers in many instances reported record business.'[15]

Special dinners were held at a number of places in Berwick including at barracks, local hospitals and the Berwick Public Assistance Institution. For many men who were spending their first Christmas in khaki, efforts were made by the townspeople to ensure that they 'felt more at home'.[16] The festivities continued on Boxing Day with the greatest success being a dance for servicemen held at the Barracks. Over 150 people attended and raised the not inconsiderable sum of £20 for the King's Own Scottish Borderers (KOSB) Comforts Fund and the Services Recreation Club. The dance continued until 1 am with musical accompaniment provided by Syd Abbott's Band, two pipers and a highland sword dancer (Lance Corporal Mortimer). Other Boxing Day attractions included a special performance of *The Drum* at the Theatre; the cinematic entertainment was hugely popular, attracting a crowd of between 400 and 500 men of the Lancashire Fusiliers.

On the railway it was reported that although there were fewer day-trippers over the holiday season the overall traffic had been very heavy with a large increase in freight and parcel traffic and a huge increase in GPO traffic. Many people from the Berwick area, however, did travel to various destinations, with Newcastle and Edinburgh being the most popular. However, the restriction of cheap travel facilities when compared with peace-time certainly resulted in a larger number than usual choosing to stay at home.

CHAPTER TWO

1940

The Year of Crisis

In Northumberland the start of the year was marked by attempts by many local councils to boost and maintain morale amongst the civilian population. Typical of these was the advert taken out in the local press by Alfred E. Green, the chairman of Amble Urban District Council. Mr Green stated that Britain would not be daunted by the efforts of the Nazis and that Amble could already boast of men in every branch of the services, showing the determination of the little town to contribute to the national war effort. Mr Green then commented on the loss of the 1,162-ton tanker SS *Amble* off Sunderland on 16 December 1939. Mr Green praised the crew (all of whom survived the vessel's mining), especially one who was in his 70s but was still determined to go back to sea to do his bit.

The Second World War saw the waters off the north east become a war zone as the Germans attempted to disrupt the vital supply lines that used the North Sea. January 21st 1940 saw two vessels sunk, one off the north

A NEW & MOMENTOUS YEAR

AMBLE DETERMINED TO PLAY ITS PART IN STRUGGLE

COUNCIL CHAIRMAN'S MESSAGE

To the People of Amble and District.

As Chairman of the Amble Urban District Council, I feel it my duty to send a word of greeting at the beginning of a new and momentous year to all the people of our urban district. When we come to contrast the New Year of 1940 with that of 1939, we cannot but be struck by the momentous changes in this short period of twelve months. A year ago we were congratulating ourselves in having so far overcome many long years of depression, the result of the world war of a quarter of a century ago.

More prosperous times we thought were to be ours in the very near future, but, alas, almost before we had time to realise the awful dangers ahead, we found ourselves confronted with a war the magnitude of which no man yet can foresee. Even at the best, it will require years of uphill work to get back to our normal life. Difficulties have to be faced, but these we are ready to meet with calm and determination.

We are going to see things through, and we of Amble are going to play our part. With but a few days warning, we were called upon to give shelter and home comfort to many hundreds of evacuees. The task seemed great, but the willingness of our people to succour those in danger and in need received them with a whole-hearted welcome. Their stay among us has been a happy one, and, as long as they remain with us, our mutual attachment will be strengthened.

Our little Amble is determined to play a big part in the struggle that lies before us. There is not a branch of His Majesty's Forces in which Amble is not taking a prominent part. Our sons met the call with a ready response.

Amble's namesake, the s.s. Amble, only a few days ago mined off the N.E. Coast, was lost, but her brave crew were rescued to a man. One of these, 74 years of age and still undaunted, has already expressed a wish to face farther hazards, if need be. Men of this calibre are ready to meet any danger. It has been reported that part of the Amble was washed ashore, a fact that justifies the remark made by one of her crew that no power could ever sink the Amble.

A spirit such as this Germany, with all her ruthlessness, will never quell. It means victory; and we are proud to know that Amble's sons are in the forefront, determined to hurl back the danger which threatens our coasts.

In the difficult times through which we are passing, I cannot but say a word of gratitude to my colleagues in the Council. Without their loyal support it would be impossible for me to shoulder the extra burdens which these abnormal times call upon us to bear.

ALFRED E. GREEN
(Chairman, Amble U.D.C.)

Amble's *Christmas and New Year message.*

The SS Amble, *sunk off Sunderland (Public Domain).*

Northumberland coast. A Latvian-owned vessel, the 4,434-ton SS *Everene*, was en route from Blyth to Liepaja when she was torpedoed by the Type IIB U-Boat *U-19* and sunk off the Farnes. One man of her thirty-one-strong crew was killed while the survivors were picked up by two fishing vessels, *Dole* and *Evesham*.[17]

Losses to U-Boats continued and just two days after the loss of the *Everene* the *U-19* claimed a further two victims in quick succession when she attacked convoy HN8 bound from Norway. *U-19* first torpedoed and sank the Norwegian vessel SS *Pluto* (1,598 tons) which was steaming off the Farnes along with the rest of the convoy. Just three minutes later the SS *Baltanglia* (1,525 tons), which had altered course to try to pick up survivors, was also hit and sunk. The men of both crews survived with those from the *Pluto* being picked up by a Finnish member of the convoy and those from *Baltanglia* managing to reach Seahouses in their lifeboats. Just two days later the *U-19* torpedoed and sank another Norwegian vessel off the Farnes, the SS *Gudveig* (1,300 tons), which was bound for Bergen from the Tyne with a cargo of coal. This time the crew were not so lucky and ten of the eighteen-man crew perished.[18]

In Alnwick there had been considerable anxiety expressed over the lack of air-raid shelters in the town compared to other towns and villages in Northumberland. Councillor Cushing stated that '[the provision of shelters] is entirely inadequate' but was rebuffed by Councillor Eltringham who said that the matter had already been put before the ARP Committee and dealt with but, as the Home Office had seen fit to declare Alnwick as being in a safe zone, any shelter provision would have to be paid for by the council and that the preparation and conversion of cellars, etc, for use as shelters was extremely expensive. The town surveyor pointed out that he estimated that there were sufficient cellars in the town to house seventy per cent of the population but that converting them all into shelters as per government regulations would be prohibitively expensive.[19]

At Berwick the lack of immediate bombing resulted in some readjustments to the local ARP organisation. It was decided that the number of full-time wardens would be reduced from 20 to 18 while the number of rescue parties was downgraded from 11 to just 6. In addition to these services there were also 128 part-time wardens and a myriad of other emergency workers. By March, school air-raid shelters had been completed and the schoolchildren were receiving training and undergoing drills on taking to the shelters quickly when the siren sounded.

Denied the chance to play a role in the newly created LDV the women in Berwickshire were also keen to do their part in the ARP services with a Women's Warden Corps being set up at Tweedmouth in May. A target number of 50 women was put in place and it took just a couple of days for the first 30 volunteers to enlist; the corps came under the command of Mrs R. Stirling of Union Park Road.

Throughout the year a number of large exercises were held to enable the ARP services to sharpen their skills and to develop new techniques. In June first aid parties from a 40-mile radius took part in an exercise in Berwick Borough which saw 100 'casualties' being dealt with. Although this was described in the local press as a 'large-scale A.R.P.

exercise' it was in fact rather limited in scope, but no doubt proved useful for the services involved.[20]

For many months the regular lecture on ARP procedures had been a popular and useful feature of wartime life in Berwick but in July the lectures at Wallace Green Hall and St. Cuthbert's RC School were discontinued and replaced with a more flexible system which gave lectures and brief demonstrations on incendiary bomb control at a variety of locations throughout the borough. The growing use of incendiary bombs and their effectiveness made it imperative that the natives of Northumberland were trained in the disposal of such items and in the extinguishing of small fires. Classes took place across the county.

Although the ARP services were both vital and appreciated by the public they came at a very high cost to the citizens and to local authorities. The initial months of the war until the end of December 1939 had cost Northumberland County Council £154,329 (some £9 million in today's money).[21] For a county such as Northumberland this was a huge amount of additional expenditure even though some of it would later be recovered from central government. The majority of the money was spent on initial building costs for shelters in the more built-up areas of the county but even largely rural north Northumberland was expensive to provide for with equipment, stores and uniforms all to be paid for along with food and other necessary supplies for the male and female volunteers.

Ambulance units were also being strengthened at this time as it became clear that the numbers of those injured in aerial attacks far outnumbered the dead, and many local corporations across Northumberland decided to invest in ambulances with Berwick taking delivery of a new and fully equipped vehicle in early July. In this case the vehicle had been provided by the County Council and was placed in the charge of Dr Agnes Sadler of Tweedmouth and Nurse Smith together with their staff from Berwick Nursing Division of the St. John's Ambulance.

Enthusiasm amongst the young who were approaching the age when they might be called up if the war went on was intense in the Berwick area with the pupils at the Grammar School forming their own Air Training Corps as early as January. So popular was the Corps that at the first meeting the first flight was formed along with the majority of a second and by the end of the first week three whole flights had been organised.

For others, enthusiasm took a rather more romantic turn and the number of marriages covered in local newspapers is noticeable at the time. Possibly people whose minds were anxiously looking at the future felt that it was better to snatch some happiness immediately rather than wait for peace and a victory which seemed far off if it was ever to come. In north Northumberland some of the more unusual wedding traditions were still adhered to and this caused some comment in the national press which was anxious to show happy times and to reassure. The *Daily Mirror* carried two stories of Northumbrian weddings. The first, in March, of Mr van Heer, was described as a fellside wedding which involved the 'Fell custom' of the bride making a leap over a 'petting stool'.[22] The second took place on 'Holy Island' (Lindisfarne). This was the wedding of 28-year-old Mary Cromarty to her childhood sweetheart Able Seaman James Hector Douglas (31) and involved not only the leaping of the stool but also a number of other 'quaint traditional rites'. These included paying a toll at the church gates to 77-year-old fisherman 'old Dick Douglas' who, the newspaper assured readers, had also received the toll from the bride's mother when she was married. This was followed by the scattering of coppers for local children by the bridegroom as he and his bride walked along the main street. On arriving at the bride's home 'a plate with a slice of wedding cake was "broken" over her head – or, rather, placed on her

Mary Cromarty married her childhood sweetheart on Holy Island (Daily Mirror).

head and then on to the ground in front of her.'[23] There was a large turnout at the event which was the first wartime wedding on the island.

With rationing at the forefront of many peoples' minds it is unsurprising that reports of poor quality meat made headlines and caused a degree of anxiety and anger. With reports of meat which was unfit for human consumption being distributed in the Rothbury area the local Food Executive Officer, Mr William N. Wade, was anxious to clarify the situation. The food collection centre at Wooler had indeed sent a batch of liver to a butcher at Longframlington which had proved to be unfit for consumption. The local Medical Officer condemned the shipment and Mr Wade passed the butcher's

Mrs Van Heer, married in rural Northumberland, undertaking the quaint custom of leaping over the petting stool (Daily Mirror).

complaint to the relevant authorities but unfortunately used the term meat instead of liver and reports had gone around the area claiming that it was 'flesh meat' which was unfit. Thus, Mr Wade was forced to publish an accurate account in the local press to assuage local fears and to assure the public that no meat which was unfit for consumption had been sold but admitted that some meat was 'rough in quality, and would not be issued to the trade in time of peace, it was all definitely sound'.[24]

At Berwick the imposition of rationing was met with a sanguine attitude as being for the best under the circumstances. The authorities reported that the residents of the district were not in the least perturbed by rationing and found that there were no shortages of items such as butter, ham and sugar and therefore there were no incidents of queuing. This situation changed rapidly as many items were added to the rationed list and shortages began to bite. As early as February the authorities were complaining of dire shortages of beef and pork (which was not at the time rationed) and were moved to complain to the local food control authorities over the fact that Berwick had been allocated only eight cattle per day (for a population of almost 7,000) with each adult permitted just 1s 10d's worth per week and children just 11d. Such was the shortage that local butchers decided to close their shops on Mondays.

Across Northumberland the rationing of petrol only to those who needed it for business purposes caused many motorists to decide not to renew their licences. In such a large and rural area like north Northumberland the petrol rationing and the laying up of motor vehicles for the duration caused some anxieties as people struggled to reach market towns on the limited bus services. It was estimated that fully a third of Northumbrian motorists had laid up their vehicles for the duration of the war as they were unable to obtain petrol vouchers (nationally the policy cost the exchequer an estimated £4,000,000 in lost revenue).

One local newspaper, the *Berwickshire News & General Advertiser*, ran a regular column entitled 'Our Children's Corner'. Written under the pseudonym 'Uncle Tom' the column attempted to both reassure, amuse and inspire children throughout the war. In February the writer of the column was clearly aware of the anxieties being suffered by both children and parents and included a poem (written by a Margaret Andrews of Eyemouth who was entertaining the troops in concerts at Berwick and across the Borders):

'For the New Year'

It's good-bye to the old and hurrah for the new,
For with promise and hope it is shining,
Though the clouds are around some are black, it is true,
If you look they've a bright silver lining.

The New Year brings tasks for us all, if you're wise,
You'll not look for worry or sorrow,
But when the morning dawns see with joys when you rise,
That here is the promised tomorrow.

The second featured poem was also a contribution from one of Uncle Tom's young club members and was a homage to the past and an effort to boost morale for the future:

'So Long Mum'

So long, Mum, just try and be brave dear;
This parting – I know how it feels,
For wasn't it here that you kissed Dad goodbye,
With me just a kid at your heels?
And didn't he ask you to smile, mum,
Because you looked worried and ill?
Remember the way he took me in his arms,
Said "Dad's off to see old Kaiser Bill!"
And now that old fellow is done with,
We'll tackle the one in his place;
Oh, Dad's son is game, and his mother's the same,
So let's show a smiling face!

A further poem featured in the column was also sent in by a member of Uncle Tom's club but was of a more stirring, martial nature:

'Ye Mariners of England'

Ye Mariners of England
That guard our native seas,
Whose flag has braved a thousand years,
The battle and the breeze!
Your Glorious standard launch again
To match another foe!
And sweep through the deep,
While the stormy winds do blow;
While the battle rages loud and long,
And the stormy winds do blow;
Britannia needs no bulwarks,
No towers along the steep;
Her march is o'er the mountain waves,
Her home is on the deep,
With thunder from the native oak,
She quells the floods below,
As the roar on the shore,
While the stormy winds do blow.

The east coast off Northumberland became a vital battleground for the supply of the nation and attacks by submarines, aircraft and the dangers of mines were commonplace at this stage of the war. On 3 February the Norwegian vessel SS *Tempo* found itself under attack by three enemy aircraft which machine-gunned the ship before returning to drop bombs, one of which struck the stern of the ship. The captain, Albert Knudsen, had a lucky escape as he was at the time having breakfast before retiring to his cabin (he had been on watch all night) which was struck by a bomb. Quickly ascertaining that the vessel was sinking Knudsen ordered the crew into the lifeboats but the German aircraft came back and attempted to machine-gun the survivors in the boats. At the subsequent inquiry into the ship's loss in Oslo Knudsen stated that the Luftwaffe crews must have known the vessel was Norwegian as she was not only flying her flag but had clear national markings on her sides (Norway was, at this point, still neutral). Knudsen and eight men were in one boat while the SS *Tempo*'s first mate and five men were in the other. After the bombers left the scene the lifeboats attempted to make for shore and the captain's boat succeeded in reaching Eyemouth where it landed safely. The second boat, however, found itself on the wrong side of Berwick's pier and capsized in the breakers after hitting rocks; of the six men aboard four drowned, one died shortly after in the harbour-master's house and one,[25] Able Seaman Olav Lillenes, survived the experience. Demonstrating the solidarity which was felt towards seamen by the people of Berwick the members of the local Rotarians entertained six of the survivors from the SS *Tempo* at their weekly luncheon.

The dangers of the wartime coasts off the north east resulted in many casualties and stories of valour and sacrifice. In February the dredger *Foremost* was attacked and sunk by German aircraft off Aberdeen. Amongst her crew was Mr Alfred Simpson (Chief Engineer) who was a former manager of a Spittal inn (the Albion). Mr Simpson, who was in his 60s, related how a direct hit rendered the dredger immobile and the order was given to abandon but one lifeboat stuck and the other capsized (the first mate and a deckhand were lost) forcing the crew to take what shelter they could aboard the dredger until the enemy was driven off at which point they were rescued by lifeboats.[26]

The Royal Navy of course proved to be a consistently popular focus of fundraising initiatives and efforts to collect comforts for the men

*The crew of an MTB disembark after a patrol along the East Coast (*Daily Mirror*).*

who were working to protect the east coast from attack. Newspapers repeatedly highlighted the work of the destroyers, minesweepers and the light fast attack boats such as the motor torpedo boats and motor gun boats; such articles were always well read in the coastal fishing communities of north Northumberland.

One local RAF squadron claimed two bombers off the coast of Northumberland on this day (3 February) with one falling into the sea off Tynemouth and another being shot down at 9.30 am (just half an hour before the attack on the SS *Tempo*) off Druridge Bay by Hurricanes of 43 Squadron based at RAF Acklington. The bodies of three of the four crewmen were recovered from the sea and buried at Chevington.[27]

Dredgers, like many other peace-time vessels, had to continue with their duties despite the added risks; the ports of the east coast had to be kept open. Just months after the experiences of Mr Simpson off Scotland the 477-ton Warkworth dredger SS *Coquetmouth* became another victim of enemy action when she struck a mine and sunk just half a mile from the harbour entrance; three of her crew were lost.[28] When the vessel struck the mine she capsized and the three men lost were trapped in the hull while the remainder of her crew were rescued by local fishing vessels. It would seem that a civilian was also killed during the incident as the civilian roll of honour lists a Mr James Brown (66) as having lost his life at the harbour entrance.

Indeed the area around the mouth of the Coquet and Coquet Island was at this time one of the most dangerous locations on the east coast and attacks were frequent and costly. However, the Luftwaffe paid a price with many of the vessels now boasting some armament and increasingly being escorted by RN vessels. On 29 March an enemy bomber attempted to attack a convoy but fell victim to the return fire of two armed trawlers which were on escort duty. The two trawlers, HMT *Rutlandshire* and HMT *Indian Star* fired machine guns and anti-aircraft guns at the bomber which crashed into Druridge Bay just a ¼ mile offshore. The police were notified and a lifeboat dispatched but found nothing but a patch of oil. The aircraft, a Junkers JU88, and three bodies were subsequently recovered. The three Luftwaffe men (Rudolf Quadt, Gustav Hartung and Andreas Wunderling) were buried at Chevington Cemetery and later the fourth member of the crew (Ernst Hesse) was buried next to them after his body washed ashore.[29]

A former journalist on the *Berwickshire News & General Advertiser*, J. Wood, who was now serving in the Royal Navy, related to his former employer how his ship's aircraft had spotted a merchant vessel which was flying neutral colours (the ship was not named due to wartime censorship).[30] The crew were suspicious and flew closer which caused the crew of the merchant vessel to take to the boats in anticipation of an attack. The aircraft then relayed its location and landed near to the vessel while its parent ship steamed at full speed to the location. Upon reaching the merchantman it was observed that the crew had embarked once again but upon being boarded the vessel was discovered to be German. The crew had attempted to scuttle the ship and the RN boarding party determined that the vessel would indeed sink. The crew were therefore

*Former reporter J. Wood wrote of his ship intercepting a German vessel (*Berwickshire News*).*

taken prisoner and transferred to the RN vessel while the British ship opened fire to destroy the merchant ship. It was then revealed that a dog and a monkey remained on board the German ship which was by now on fire. The dog jumped overboard and began swimming towards the British ship which ceased fire and one of the German crew volunteered to enter the water to rescue the animal. Having done so successfully the German captain was observed to be in tears when he was reunited with his pet![31]

The village of Otterburn, on the Northumberland moors, was pitched into a state of excitement when one of its natives captained a destroyer which successfully sank a German U-Boat in the Irish Sea (reports from the time claim that he sunk two in half an hour but the second never seems to have been confirmed). Returning home to Otterburn Tower on leave Lieutenant Commander Richard P. White was accorded a hero's welcome by the village. Flags and bunting were strung across the main street and the entire population of the village turned out to welcome him home. The local schoolchildren were well to the fore with flags and pictures of antelopes (for reasons that will become clear) and U-Boats being sunk. Other posters declared

'Welcome Home' and 'Well Bowled', complete with shattered stumps formed by U-Boats (a reference to his family's well-known cricketing connections), and the happy children were given the day off in celebration. The children of Otterburn had been working on their banners and collecting their pennies ever since they had found out that it was Commander White's ship that had been successful. Upon arriving at the driveway to Otterburn Tower the lieutenant commander's car (with him and his wife inside) was pulled by rope up the drive by local men to his doorstep where the vicar waited to welcome him home. The hero was presented with a silver cigarette case on behalf of the children of Otterburn by local child Leslie Gleig who said that he and his fellow children of Otterburn asked

Captain White, RN.

*Captain White being pulled up the driveway by local volunteers (*Daily Mirror*).*

that the commander accept the gift because they were 'proud of you'.[32]

The lieutenant commander was officer in command of HMS *Antelope*, an A-class destroyer which had been built on the Tyne. On 5 February, *Antelope* was the only escort for the outward-bound convoy OA84 and was off the southern coast of Ireland when the German submarine *U-41* launched a torpedo attack on the convoy sinking the freighter SS *Beaverburn* and damaging the tanker SS *Ceronia*. Lieutenant Commander White steered HMS *Antelope* towards the U-Boat and launched a depth charge attack which sank the enemy submarine with all hands.[33] White remained modest about his achievements and in a short address to the villagers stated that he had 'done nothing, nothing at all'.

He had two brothers who were also in the forces.[34] His father, Sir Archibald W. White was a skilled cricketer who had captained Yorkshire from 1911-14 (winning the title in 1912) while the lieutenant

Captain White was given a raucous greeting and presentation at Otterburn (Daily Mirror).

HMS Antelope *(Public Domain).*

commander had played for Northumberland (one of his brothers was captain).

Although there was widespread sympathy for the plight of evacuees this did not always extend to a warm welcome. Berwick Town Council was alarmed at being classified as a reception area and expected to house 500 evacuees. The council gained the support of the local MP, Sir Hugh Seely, and approached the Ministry to attempt to get the town reclassified. The Ministry, unsurprisingly, refused to change the classification and ordered the council to make immediate preparations to house the evacuees and to make ready emergency hostels to house an expected five per cent of the evacuees who would be 'unsuitable for billeting in private households' (mainly due to their health or standards of hygiene).[35] The Ministry assured the council that it would provide suitable funds for such centres. The council had already undertaken a survey of empty housing in the town and had secured a large house for the use of twenty-five evacuees.

Although Alnwick had rallied around the evacuees in 1939, by January 1940 it had become increasingly clear that space had run out and that there were no more volunteers coming forward to house the extra evacuees. This was despite the authorities believing many people did still have sufficient space to house the extra evacuees. As a result, it was decided that the only way forward was to bring in a system of compulsion which would force those with space to house evacuees. The first step was the creation of an evacuation tribunal which would meet to sort through cases and make out the necessary orders. There was some opposition to the new system which would see an Evacuation Officer order householders to house evacuees and if they refused they would be called before the tribunal and, if they still refused, possibly prosecuted. One councillor, Mr Hindmarsh, stated that he would be reluctant to support the measure as, to him, 'it savours too much of Germany'.[36] However, he was eventually persuaded after Councillors Cushing and Eltringham assured him that the voluntary system had failed and that on numerous occasions householders had flatly refused to take in evacuees. The meeting adopted the new procedure but also praised the majority of Alnwick residents for their acceptance of the unfortunate evacuees. The committee heard that a large number of evacuees had returned home for the Christmas holidays but that almost all of them had now returned to Alnwick.

The influx of evacuees caused considerable dislocation to the education and healthcare system of towns across Northumberland with councils being asked to cobble together responses as and when need arose and in response to demands from the Ministry of Health office in Newcastle. In Alnwick the council was ordered to requisition Barndale House for conversion into a hospital for evacuees with the costs being met by the government.

As the war entered its second year, many Northumbrians had been left puzzled by the lack of military action and the Phoney War (also commonly known as the Bore War) had become a topic of much debate on the streets with some expressing the hope that the war could be halted. Such hopes were dashed however when Germany invaded Norway and Denmark in April. The British response to the invasion of Norway was an organisational shambles and a demoralised British force was forced to retreat. The Norwegian campaign had huge ramifications including a two-day debate in the House of Commons which resulted in Neville Chamberlain narrowly winning a vote of confidence but losing his mandate to continue as Prime Minister. After talks with his own party and the Labour Party leadership, Chamberlain resigned on 10 May.

Berwick's MP, Captain McEwen, stated at a meeting in his home constituency that he did not view the Norway campaign as a disaster but that severance from the French would indeed be a disaster. Showing a failure to grasp the public mood, which was increasingly suspicious of the poor disclosure of war news by the government, Captain McEwen stated that the two-day debate in parliament 'had been very regrettable. It was not proper to "wash dirty linen" in public', he was forced to admit however that if the meeting had been held in secret 'the people would have said there was something to hide'. McEwen, again flying against overwhelming public opinion, stated that he was still a firm supporter of Mr Chamberlain but conceded that the new Prime Minister, Churchill, was a patriot who would put his country first. In an effort to analyse the situation Captain McEwen again demonstrated just how ignorant the British authorities were in their assumptions about their French allies. He referred to the French as possessing 'the best land force in the world'; events in France were about to show that he was very wrong.[37]

On the same day that Britain lost its Prime Minister, the Germans crossed the border into Belgium and Holland and, using fast moving tank columns backed up by supporting airpower and artillery, made massive and rapid gains. In the south the German blitzkrieg pushed through Luxembourg and the Ardennes Forest to bypass the much-vaunted Maginot Line and the Germans reached the coast in just eleven days, cutting off the BEF in the north. Despite brave and indeed heroic resistance, the BEF was forced back and it became clear that unless an evacuation could be made Britain would lose the majority of her Army.

The news of the events in France and the Low Countries was met with barely suppressed horror amongst the civilian population of Northumberland and there were widespread recriminations against the perceived mismanagement of the Chamberlain government. Nevertheless morale was reported to be holding and as it became clear that the evacuations from Dunkirk had been successful beyond anyone's imagining a feeling grew of determination to oppose Hitler and Nazism no matter what.

Like many other local publications, the *Berwick Advertiser* praised the events at Dunkirk and described the 'deep feeling of thankfulness' at the successful evacuation of much of the BEF, including many men from the local area. The newspaper related how the families of 'Berwick men serving with the BEF went about their work at the week-end with light hearts and smiling faces'. It also explained how the news of those who had been brought safely back to Britain was relayed to anxious relatives in telegrams, postcards and telephone calls and how the news spread throughout the town by word of mouth with one man whose son had been evacuated claiming, 'I feel like a new man. It's great news: the best I have ever had!'[38]

Amongst the accounts that emerged from local men who had been brought off the beaches was that of Driver N. Richardson of Berwick. Although the RAF (unfairly) came in for criticism over its actions at Dunkirk , Driver Richardson was anxious to lavish praise on them telling readers of the *Berwick Advertiser* that he had seen four RAF fighters attack a much larger fleet of enemy bombers and shoot down four of them; he concluded by saying, 'There is no doubting the fact that our boys are on top in the air.' Although Driver Richardson played down the risks he had taken, both in the retreat and the evacuation, and described the British Army as being in good order, he did admit, not unreasonably, that it was 'great to be back in England just the same'.[39]

Another Berwick member of the Royal Army Service Corps (RASC), Driver Robert Christopher Carr, related his experiences in a rather bleaker manner. During his interview with his local newspaper he stated how he had witnessed German aircraft bombing and machine-gunning hundreds of refugees, mainly women and children, on the St. Pol-Bethune road and how when he and his comrades were wading and swimming to British vessels at Dunkirk the Luftwaffe would repeatedly strafe the men in the water causing great casualties.

The family of Private Robert Craik were anxious but relieved to hear that he had been successfully evacuated back to Britain but that he had been bayoneted in the leg during hand-to-hand fighting. By the time news of the successful evacuation of Dunkirk had broken, Private Craik was recuperating at home in Berwick.

Despite the reports of light hearts and smiling faces, not every family received good news. The parents of Sergeant David Borthwick, RAF, received tragic news at their Walkergate, Berwick, home when a telegram arrived informing them that their son had been posted missing in France. Sergeant Borthwick had been in the RAF for almost eleven years and on 16 May was flying as an observer in an 18 Squadron Blenheim IV aircraft tasked with reconnaissance of the advancing German army. After taking off from Poix nothing further was heard and the aircraft was shot down some 8 km south-south-east of Cambrai; all three crewmen were killed. Sergeant Borthwick was an old boy of Berwick Grammar School and was aged 26 when he lost his life.[40]

Henry George Alan Percy, the 9th Duke of Northumberland, was at the time serving in France as a Lieutenant in 3rd Battalion, Grenadier Guards. By 20 May the position of the BEF was precarious in that while the majority attempted to hold off the German advance in the north they were endangered by a successful German attack in the south which threatened to engulf them. The commanders were unsure of the exact position and continued to send out positive encouragement about the general situation. Flanked by Belgian and French troops, seven divisions of British troops were ordered to hold the line at the canalised River Escaut and the River Scheldt. The next morning a German barrage opened up on the positions held by 3rd Grenadier Guards to the east of Bailleul. Despite the severe shelling, British troops attempted valiantly to hold off the Germans but were quickly in danger of being overrun. The commander of 4 Company, Major Reggie

Alston-Roberts-West, and Lieutenant Percy went forward to ascertain the situation and managed to rescue the wounded Lieutenant Nigel Forbes (the Master of Forbes) before once again going forward, Major Alston-Roberts-West having decided to contact Battalion HQ to organise a counter-attack.

By 11.30 am a counter-attack was developed by 3 Company (which had been held in reserve at HQ) and despite some initial success (after some displays of great, almost foolhardy, courage) losses were very high. Lieutenant Percy was leading a platoon on the right of the attack when his courage got the better of him and he became the most famous of the county's casualties. It has been said that 'the Duke of Northumberland ... bravely, but rashly, failed to take cover, preferring to stand up in the face of German fire, so that he could wave his men forward with his ash stick'.[41] The counter-attack was so ferocious that the Germans were forced to retreat back behind the river.

The Duke's actions were very widely praised at the time and it would certainly seem that, rather than waving his men forward with his stick like some officers did in the early years of the First World War, he fell after being responsible for stabilising a very dangerous situation; in the immediate aftermath of the action in which the Duke died his company commander wrote:

> The attack had just developed when the right forward platoon, commanded by Lieutenant the Duke of Northumberland came under heavy machine-gun fire from the front and right flank. Northumberland, realizing the danger, led his platoon forward with great gallantry and reached the objective.
>
> The enemy machine-guns in this sector were silenced and the guns put out of action. During the consolidation Northumberland was hit through the neck and back by enemy machine-gun fire from a position in depth beyond the first objective.
>
> His gallant leadership in a critical situation greatly helped to restore the line and ultimately the Germans withdrew to the other side of the river.[42]

Two days later the BEF retreated once more and because of heavy casualties could not recover many of its fallen. A Hauptmann (Captain) Lothar Ambrosius described how he and his men recovered and buried the bodies of approximately sixty men and officers from the Grenadier Guards, amongst them those of Lieutenant Percy and Major Alston-Roberts-West. Henry George Alan Percy was aged 27 at the time of his death. He had been seen as one of Britain's most eligible bachelors and remained unmarried at the time of his death. Described as being tall and good looking with sandy hair the Duke had travelled widely and had a well-earned reputation for his skill in fox-hunting and chess. The residents of Alnwick and indeed all Northumberland mourned his loss; he was renowned and respected as a generous landlord and a highly intelligent and able

Lieutenant Henry George Alan Percy, killed during the retreat to Dunkirk (Public Domain).

young man. Before the war he had been joint Master of the Percy Hunt, a Justice of the Peace, a member of the County Council, and had been Parliamentary Secretary to the Lord Privy Seal and Parliamentary Secretary to the Secretary of State for Air. His body was recovered and subsequently interred at Esquelmes War Cemetery.

The Duchess was informed of her son's death at her home of Lesbury House and ordered that the Percy flag (the blue lion rampant) be flown at half-mast from Alnwick Castle. The Castle was at the time being used by evacuees from Newcastle's Church High School as it had been closed down in 1939 as a result of the £1,000,000 estimated death duties which had accrued as a result of the death of the 8th Duke. George was succeeded as 10th Duke of Northumberland by his unmarried brother Hugh Algernon Percy who was at the time a subaltern in the Northumberland Hussars.

Just days after the Duke's death news came through that 34-year-old Captain Robert William Armstrong, 9th (Machine-Gun) Battalion, Royal Northumberland Fusiliers, had been killed in action during the retreat to Dunkirk. Captain Armstrong had previously been the manager of the Royal Assurance Company, Berwick branch, and lived at the Meadows, Berwick-upon-Tweed. Captain Armstrong was well-known in the town where he was a Rotarian. Captain Armstrong died of wounds sustained during his unit's action to stem the German breakthrough and protect the Dunkirk area.

The 9th Battalion had been dispatched to France in April as part of the 23 (Northumbrian) Division. The division was established as a motorized one but was sent to France as a digging unit for labour tasks only; this was because the division was only partly trained and equipped at the time. When the Germans broke through the French lines on 17 May the French asked if the 23rd Division could be used to man defences along the Canal du Nord. It was this request that first alerted the British to the extent of the disaster which had occurred. The request was duly granted and the division moved to positions on the canal. They were ordered to defend a frontage of sixteen miles, were outflanked and were faced with five enemy panzer divisions.

Upon arriving at the 'canal' the commanding officer of 1st Tyneside Scottish (Black Watch, Royal Highland Regiment), part of the 23rd, Lieutenant Colonel Hugh Swinburne, was horrified to discover that the canal was in fact dry and amounted to only a shallow ditch which would prove little obstacle to the enemy panzers. Left with no alternative, the men of the 23rd Division did their best and began a fighting retreat towards Arras but, unsurprisingly, suffered very heavy casualties in the process.

Amongst the Northumbrian casualties suffered by 9th Northumberland Fusiliers during the fight for France and the subsequent evacuation of the BEF from Dunkirk was Captain Ernest Benjamin Lomas Hart, aged 33. Hart was the only son of Colonel E.J. Hart OBE and Mrs Hart of Rothbury and was married to Beatrice (Peggy) Hart. Captain Hart lost his life on 24 May and has no known grave, being commemorated on the Dunkirk Memorial.

The fate of 9th Royal Northumberland Fusiliers shocked Northumberland but worse was to follow in the aftermath of the 'miracle' of Dunkirk when local newspapers began to report confused accounts of the fate of another Royal Northumberland Fusiliers battalion (it turns out to have been the 7th (Territorial) RNF, the 'parent' battalion of the 9th, which had been attached to 51st (Highland) Division as a machine-gun battalion). Although confused and vague about the details, the reports were clear that the battalion had suffered a dreadful fate. Early accounts stated that the battalion (and the division to which it was attached) had faced off against an overwhelming German force and that many, reports stated over 6,000, had been taken prisoner after being cut off from rescue at St. Valery. The account given in the *Berwick Advertiser* was typical in that it claimed that the battalion had made history but admitted that the full story was not yet known, adding that 'already many of the officers and men of this battalion have been officially reported as missing. Parents have been awaiting for some weeks news of their sons, great anxiety prevailing for their safety.'[43] The account, in an attempt to bolster morale in the face of this loss, stated that 'the full story of their valour is not yet known [but the stand of the battalion] ... will rank as one of the most gallant against fearful odds which has been known in British history.' Other accounts compared the actions of the division and the Northumbrians who were a part of it to the gallantry displayed during the Charge of the Light Brigade.

Those taken prisoner included the commanding officer of the battalion, Lieutenant Colonel G.E. Fenwicke-Clennell,[44] and the adjutant, Captain D.V. Brims. Captain Brims was a well-known sportsman in Northumberland having captained Morpeth Cricket Club, played hockey for the county and golf at Alnmouth, where he resided.

Two of the other officers from the 7th RNF who were taken prisoner were also well-known Northumbrian sportsmen. Captain Jack Fawcus was a professional jockey from Chathill and had been the country's leading amateur jockey in 1931-32 (when he rode fifty-four winners) and finished second in the 1937 Grand National aboard Coolean. Indeed Jack became a very skilled rider of the National: riding in the race nine times he recorded finishes of 2nd, 3rd (aboard 66/1 outsider Batchelor Prince) and 4th (twice). Jack also recorded three victories in the Scottish national (two aboard Southern Hero (1934 and 1939)) and won the King George's Chase at Kempton in 1937 (again on Southern Hero). Captain Fawcus was also renowned as a fine shot and held a wide interest in other sports. He was reported to be in tears at the surrender and gave his captors a very hard time, attempting to escape on several occasions. While at camp VI-B Fawcus was one of many officers who escaped by tunnel but was subsequently recaptured. When recaptured by local units many of the men ended up being entertained by German country-folk, the majority of whom treated them very well while they awaited pick-up by the authorities. In return, they gave them their Red Cross food supplies, which were most welcome as many had not seen items such as chocolate for years. There were stories that local villagers and children followed the lorries with the prisoners throwing food from the back! Obviously the Germans were unimpressed by this and the men were incarcerated in a damp dungeon and badly treated before being shipped off to Colditz. Jack, as a jockey, was already thin, and he was very ill by the time he reached Colditz; he had been refused medical treatment earlier. His ill-health proved to be so severe that he was repatriated to Britain in 1943.[45]

Jack Fawcus in his pre-war career as a jockey; he was captured and imprisoned at Colditz (Public Domain).

The other renowned sportsman was Captain R.J. Middlemas of Alnwick who before the war had gained fame as one of the best rifle shots in the country. Middlemas had shot at the Northumberland Rifle Meeting, at Bisley and the King's Hundred; a married former Cambridge man he had also shot in Canada with a public schools' team.

One more grimly humorous incident to come out of the disasters which had impacted the two RNF battalions was that experienced by Fusilier John Bain, a butcher in his civilian life, of St. Aidan's Road, Berwick. Returning to his parental home on leave, Fusilier Bain discovered a letter in the letterbox addressed to his mother. When his mother opened the letter it proved to be a note telling her that her son, who was standing in front of her, and had indeed handed her the letter, was missing in action! John had a brother in the RNF who was also home on leave at the time and there had obviously been some confusion. Greatly amused by the incident John took the note back with him as a souvenir.[46]

Despite the success of the evacuation, the losses suffered by the two battalions and the mass surrender cast a pall of gloom over many Northumberland communities. The small north Northumberland hamlet of Haggerston, for example, was home to one family which was anxiously awaiting news of three brothers. John, Tom and Peter Arnott had given up their respective careers of greengrocer, park-keeper and gardener to join territorial battalions of the Royal Northumberland Fusiliers and were mobilised two days before war was declared. Their parents received three separate telegrams notifying them that their sons were missing; the entire community anxiously awaited further news. In December news eventually came through that the brothers were prisoners of war and that two of them were in the same camp along with two of their friends, the Hattle brothers of Fenwick near Berwick. All five of the men were being employed on farms by the Germans and reported that they were in good health.[47]

The actions at St. Valery saw the award of the Distinguished Service Medal to one Berwick seaman. Robert Taylor, RN, earned the highly respected medal for his actions in the abortive attempts to evacuate elements of the 51st Division from the small port and beach at the French town. A former grocer, Robert had always been a keen sailor and had spent his holidays working on a small fishing boat. When war broke out he joined the Royal Navy and was posted to a minesweeper. Seaman Taylor related to his local newspaper the events that led to the award. After collecting their first load of soldiers from St. Valery under heavy artillery fire Seaman Taylor's minesweeper set course for Le Havre to transfer the Tommies. On the way the ship came under aerial attack from a dive bomber which the minesweeper's gunners drove off damaged. Returning from Le Havre to St. Valery, Seaman Taylor volunteered to man a lifeboat tasked to go in under cover of darkness to pick up troops from the beach. On his fifth trip his lifeboat was hit by enemy fire and broke in half depositing Seaman Taylor in the sea. He promptly swam to a deserted lifeboat and rescued more troops but on the return trip noticed in the growing light that the British fleet was preparing to depart (it had been decided at this point that further evacuations were impossible). Continuing to row towards the departing fleet Seaman Taylor noticed his own minesweeper moving close into shore searching for him but on finding no sign of him he saw it leaving to rejoin the main fleet. Seaman Taylor reported that he was undaunted by this development and began rowing towards a French trawler. The French vessel took the men on board and sailed, under attack, to Cherbourg where Seaman Taylor was able to make himself known to the naval authorities. After hearing that he had been posted missing, he secured a berth for himself and the soldiers he had rescued aboard a destroyer to Britain. Seaman Taylor then rejoined his ship in England, a scene which he described as being 'a joyous re-union, because my mates thought I had been lost'.[48] On his subsequent leave, suffering from a hand injury, Seaman Taylor not only enjoyed the praise of his townsfolk but also married Katie Whillis, the daughter of a local motor haulage contractor.

There was sad news when the wife of Berwick soldier Driver George Norman Turnbull revealed that he had died in a military hospital in southern England. Driver Turnbull was a member of the RASC and, like many, had been cut off from his unit during the retreat to Dunkirk. After he had been landed in Britain his wife managed to get to his side and he related many of his experiences to her. Amongst these were how he had shot a German paratrooper and how, during the retreat, he had endured severe privation which led to him falling ill and that he had waited for a boat for five days out in the open with no food and little water. The doctor who had operated on Driver Turnbull described him as 'the bravest patient they had ever had' but, sadly, Turnbull could not recover. He died and was buried in his hometown cemetery.[49] Turnbull had been a regular soldier for nine years and was called up at the outbreak of war, which he met with great cheerfulness.

*Seaman Robert Taylor was awarded the Distinguished Service Medal for his courage in evacuating soldiers from France (*Berwickshire News*).*

Those manning the vessels which were attempting to lift the BEF from the French coast were an inviting target and many paid with their lives. Amongst them was 32-year-old Berwick man Leading Seaman David Burgon, RNR (Patrol Service), who was killed when the trawler HMT *Blackburn Rovers* was sunk. The news was deeply felt as Burgon (better known as Davy) was well known, well liked and widely respected, especially in the Low Greens area which had been his home for all of his life. Many of his friends in the Pilot Inn drank a silent toast to his memory upon hearing the news.[50]

Another Berwick man, a veteran of the First World War, was serving at Dunkirk aboard the minesweeper HMT *Boy Roy* when she was sunk by enemy action. Thankfully the sailor survived the experience but, typically, was modest about the experiences which he had been a part of saying only that 'The Merchant Navy and fishermen who manned small craft all did more than their share.'[51]

After the evacuation of Dunkirk, a small amount of time was given to relieved celebration, although the Prime Minister quickly moved to ensure that the people of Britain were aware of the realities of the

His Majesty's Trawler Blackburn Rovers, *sunk at Dunkirk (Public Domain).*

situation facing them, namely that an invasion attempt was now likely. Many people were demanding to be given a more active role in the defence of Britain, so it was little surprise when on 14 May the government announced the creation of the Local Defence Volunteers (LDV).

The inhabitants of the Berwick area were said to have been most enthusiastic to answer the call to service. The first attested member of the force in Berwick was Mr W.L. McCreath of Castle Terrace and the second was Mr M.H. Blackett of local drapers Rutherford & Blackett. On that first day only sixteen men (approximately 0.23% of the town's population) came forward (compared to 464 in North Shields, representing approximately 0.7% of the total population of North Shields and Tynemouth). But after two days there were 220 volunteers.

The growing threat of invasion led to the commencement of a defence building programme and metal and concrete obstacles began to appear in fields around Northumberland to discourage enemy aircraft (especially gliders) from landing. At Berwick large poles were erected on the Shad and at the Border Bridge while barbed wire was placed on the quayside. Trenches (both for defence and to prevent aircraft landing) were dug behind the pier and on the golf course. To enable important road intersections to be controlled, concrete roadblocks were erected along with defensive positions at the local bridges, including the Royal Tweed Bridge.

Recruitment in Berwick continued to be somewhat sporadic and when recruitment was suspended in July in areas where the force was up to strength Berwick was not included as its force was still below the acceptable level. A further appeal brought forward only another fifteen men, ten of whom were former servicemen.

The biggest change for the force came also in July when it was decided, at the prompting of Churchill, to rename the force from the perceived sedentary LDV to something a little more forceful; thus the LDV became known as the Home Guard. This change aided recruitment in parts of Northumberland as it eliminated some of the misconceptions that the LDV was a useless force. It was the butt of many jokes, the most famous being that LDV stood for 'Look, Duck and Vanish'. The renaming, along with the support of prominent politicians, ensured the speeding up of equipping the force. This resulted in a boost in morale and, given the increasing possibility of invasion throughout the summer, the Home Guardsmen's duties were increasingly appreciated.

In December a Berwick Home Guard, Harold Thompson, was fined £2 for failing to appear on parade; this was the first such case in Berwick. Mr Thompson had been discharged from the Army in April and had subsequently joined the Home Guard but on the night in question he had an argument at home and was left with nowhere to sleep for the night. He claimed it was this circumstance which made him miss parade but he was told, in addition to his fine, that the matter had been put in the hands of his battalion commander and that a decision would be made on whether he would be discharged or not.

Lack of equipment and lack of training facilities were the most common problems for the LDV/Home Guard, especially as the force grew, and many ingenious solutions were found. Immediately upon the call, the Berwick British Legion Shooting Club decided to make available its equipment, facilities and firing range to the force, and this made a huge difference to it. 'Many very busy nights were spent on the miniature range … up to 40 members of the Home Guard receiving instruction on a single night.'[52] The volunteers enjoyed the experience but had to pay for their ammunition as the club simply could not afford this expense. The situation did not last long as the government quickly made ammunition available to the services and the Home Guard.

The formation of the Home Guard had encouraged an interest in shooting in many Berwick residents and a large number of people had expressed an interest in joining the club. These included a number of women (the membership was at that point all male) who wished to learn accurately to fire a rifle in case of invasion.[53] The annual meeting of the club concluded with the decision to temporarily disband the club due to the number of members who had joined the forces and the lack of ammunition in the future. A large number of members had indeed joined the services (one had already been taken prisoner) including the honorary secretary and treasurer Mr J.E. Learmonth and the vice-captain and match secretary Mr S. Hay, both of whom had joined the RAF.[54]

People in northern Northumberland were wary of the possibility of enemy parachute landings (much of the anxiety bolstered by scare stories from France and the Low Countries). The primary role of the Home Guard was to report and hold out against such attacks, and commanders were aware of the vast amount of open and thinly populated countryside for which they were responsible. To help them in their efforts it was decided to solicit the aid of those who were for whatever reason unable to join the Home Guard to volunteer as watchers. Adverts were placed in the press calling for such volunteers in Berwickshire, Roxburghshire and Selkirkshire (including Berwick itself) with similar adverts appearing in parts of rural Northumberland. The adverts specifically mentioned that women would be accepted in the role.[55]

The platoon commander in Berwick, E.D. Mackay, announced that the Home Guard had been given permission to recruit many more members and that it would particularly welcome ex-servicemen with previous military experience. However, young men would also be enrolled and trained and Mackay was at pains to point out that young men who would almost certainly be called up in the future would benefit greatly from Home Guard training and that they would be protecting their homes and families.

Indeed, one of the main successes of the Home Guard was in giving initial military drill training and weapons drill to many men who went on to join the regular forces. John Moffett from Berwick was one such man. A bank accountant, Mr Moffett was a keen sportsman and a member of many clubs in Berwick. He had represented Northumberland in rowing while also being a keen amateur dramatist. Mr Moffett had joined the Home Guard at its inception and in August he was commissioned in the RAF.

Defences were quickly constructed around the vulnerable coastlines of Britain and were further developed while the threat remained (throughout 1940-42). Of particular concern in Northumberland was Druridge Bay which features a large gently sloping sandy beach backed by sand dunes pierced at several points by small streams allowing access off the beach to the road and coastal farmland beyond. The site was seen as being 'exceptionally vulnerable to an enemy landing [and was] … the most critical point (the Centre Sub-Sector of No 2 Sector) in the defence positions occupied by 162 Infantry Brigade'.[56]

The 162nd Infantry Brigade, under the command of Brigadier J. Macready and, from the end of August, Brigadier R.B.S. Reford, was responsible for the defence of the entire Northumberland coast and was thus spread quite thin, but it was bolstered by local Home Guard units. A territorial formation and part of the 54th (East Anglian) Infantry Division (another territorial unit) the brigade included: 6th Battalion, Bedfordshire and Hertfordshire Regiment; 1st Battalion, Hertfordshire Regiment; 2nd Battalion, Hertfordshire Regiment; and 162nd Infantry Brigade Anti-Tank Company. The defences at Druridge Bay were extensive and included minefields, anti-tank ditches, pillboxes, sandbagged positions, anti-tank blocks, beach scaffolding (with mines), and anti-tank artillery positions.

Other defences included the establishment of a number of so-called 'stop lines' which ran along several Northumbrian rivers and other natural features. These were the Coquet stop line which ran from upper Coquetdale to Amble, the Wansbeck stop line which ran to the west and east of Morpeth, the Alnwick-Wooler stop line, and the Belford-Wooler stop line. The small town of Wooler was at the meeting point of two stop lines and as such came to be seen as an important part of the defence network of Northumberland. In 1940 the defended village of Wooler was manned by the men of 162nd Brigade but they were replaced in 1941 and the defences upgraded.

As we have seen, Alnwick housed a large number of evacuees, but the fact that many had returned home when enemy bombing did not happen immediately resulted in problems in the summer of 1940 when the Battle of Britain was in progress. In early June, Alnwick War Emergency Committee was forced to report to the district council that the town had been asked immediately to house a further 400 evacuees from Tyneside. Having learnt from the experience of 1939 that the splitting of the town into just eleven or twelve areas was too unwieldy, it was agreed that this time the town would be split into forty smaller districts which would mean that each billeting officer would only be responsible for one or two streets. The voluntary returns of those who were willing to take in evacuees clearly points to a split in attitudes: eighty per cent of those who responded to the request were those who were already housing evacuees.

Another troubling problem in June was the declaration of war by Italy on the 10th. There were significant numbers of Italians and persons of Italian descent in Britain; indeed there were some in Northumberland. They were now classed as enemy aliens and the authorities acted quickly to round them up for assessment and probable interment. Many of the Italians in Northumberland were shop owners with many owning confectioners' and/or fish and chip shops. Antonio (Tony) Corvie owned a fish and chip shop at 33 West Street and had lived in Berwick for many years. Tony had married a Berwick woman and the couple had a young child at school in the town. Tony's shop was so popular that he later opened a second shop on Railway Street. Just hours after the declaration of war the police visited Tony and he was detained. That night his shop in Railway Street was attacked by an unknown group who threw a brick through one of the front windows. The other family to suffer through no fault of their own was that of Carl Forte. Forte also owned two shops in the town: a fish and chip shop at 5 Walkergate and a confectioner's at 15 Hide Hill. Forte was likewise detained and a mob attacked one of his premises; the shop on Hide Hill, which had several windows smashed, had to be boarded up. These were just the first of several incidents. Over the next few hours the police detained 'other Italians' and 'most of the Italian shops in Berwick were closed from Tuesday onwards'. The local press reported that 'shortages of ice-cream were indeed one of the inconveniences which the Berwick people cheerfully suffered during the round-up. Ice-cream carts and barrows stood in yards, lonely and forlorn, without the usual clutter of people around them. British owners of fish and chip restaurants in the town report a big increase in business.'[57]

As in the previous war, there was a determined attempt to reduce wastage of materials. Metals, glass, paper and cloth were added to a list of items which the people of Northumberland should save. Rationing of several of these items was already in force with paper becoming a rationed item in February. Rothbury Rural District Council mounted a local advertising campaign urging surrounding villages to donate these items as part of a scavenging campaign which, it was claimed, would benefit the war effort. The Controller of Salvage was at particular pains to urge the saving of paper as, with the fall of Denmark and Norway, a major supply of wood pulp had been disrupted. The council was urged to oversee the creation of collecting centres in every village in Coquetdale.

When the 'Go To It!' appeal was made by Mr Bevin for the donation and collection of metal, especially aluminium and iron, the people of Berwick entered into the spirit with enthusiasm. The local press reported that Berwick residents had the satisfaction of knowing that the metals which they contributed on the town's first salvage day held on 17 July would soon 'be flying above them in the form of fighter planes or [would be] ... part of a gun or some such useful weapon'.[58] Of course, this was seldom true; the majority of collected metal was not of sufficient quality to be utilised in such a manner.

However, the collection day was a resounding success, demonstrating the patriotism of Berwick's citizens. The people of the town had been preparing for a week by going through their yards, sheds and attics looking for suitable items and many housewives gave pots and pans which had hardly been used, such was their enthusiasm. There were several odd donations which were collected by corporation workmen including a heavy garden roller which was donated by one gentlemen and which was loaded with great difficulty. One old lady who feared she had no metal or other items to give decided to put some fine old jewellery up for auction with the proceeds going to the war effort and, upon hearing of this, several other residents of the town decided to follow her lead with one commenting, 'I cannot fight, but by jove, I intend giving all I can to stop these Nazis reaching Britain!'[59]

When finally tallied, the collection had taken in a huge amount of material from what was a relatively small town. One local scrap dealer could not believe that the town which he had worked in for so many years could have produced such a vast collection.

Results of Berwick's First Salvage Day Collection	
Item	**Amount Collected**
Scrap iron	12 tons
Aluminium	2,000 pieces
Tin	4 tons
Paper and cardboard	5½ tons
Cloth rags	4 tons
Glass bottles	960
Brass	2 cwt

Charitable collections for the services and collections aimed at the purchase of military equipment and supplies were immensely popular, especially as the Battle of Britain raged and the invasion shadow loomed over Northumberland. Berwick-upon-Tweed set up, along with many other local towns and villages, its own Spitfire Fund in an effort to raise the money required to purchase one of the famous fighter aircraft for the defence of Britain. A well-known local bowler, Mrs Lamb of Church Square, came up with the inspiring idea of collecting a mile of pennies. A final target of raising £5,000 was also agreed upon. The newly established fund urged people to collect twelve pennies and post them in. Some other places were asking for donations of shillings but it was decided pennies would enable everyone to join in and hopefully boost the fund's popularity. A dance in the Drill Hall was quickly organised to provide an initial boost for the fund. In the following weeks it was agreed to pool the fundraising efforts and to attempt to raise money for a Berwick and North Northumberland Spitfire Fund.

Alongside the Home Guard was another, far more secretive, group of men who had sworn to defend Britain in the event of invasion. Little if anything was known about these men as each was bound by the Official Secrets Act not to talk of their duties, even to their families. They were the men of the Auxiliary Units who would, in the event of invasion, go underground (quite literally as each unit had underground bases in their area of operation) before resurfacing to sow havoc amongst the Germans with ambushes, assassinations, sabotage and the reporting of German positions. There were several such units in Northumberland including one which was based in the vicinity of Longhorsley. However, it was not until after the war that one man, a child during the war, revealed to a former member that he had, along with several friends, discovered the base concealed by the roots of a tree and that they had often explored it (not knowing that it was full of explosives and ammunition!). The same gentleman also discovered, although not until after the war, that a neighbour who lived in the old tower in the village had a secret radio station (most likely connected with the Auxiliaries) which was frequently visited by the local priest, Father Wright.[60]

The residents of Wooler were extremely keen and continued to raise funds throughout the summer and autumn by holding a house-to-house collection, a whist drive and a dance at Archbold Hall which would be hosted by the RAMC band. Mr Milton Simpson of Yearle House had already donated a cheque for £500 and urged others to be generous. In late September a flag day was held and a coffee and biscuit morning, organised by Miss Margaret Jaboor, was well supported, raising over £7.

As the year entered its final month many began to review what had possibly been the most trying year in Britain's history. Efforts to continue to raise funds for the war effort continued and many communities released details of how much money they had contributed throughout 1940. Rothbury Rural District, for example, could point out that the community had successfully contributed £28,844 5s 10d to the War Savings campaign up until the end of September and expected to have raised a similar sum over the rest of the year.

Crime

Minor crimes continued to be prosecuted zealously and there was a rash of driving offences in the early spring. One driver, Miss Violet Davidson (of Alnwick), found herself charged with driving without due care after an incident in Amble which would have resulted in a serious collision had it not been for the skilful driving of another motorist. Miss Davidson had been driving a car in the village at just before 10 am and when proceeding from Bridge Street into Queen Street she had attempted to overtake a coal wagon without checking if anything was approaching from the opposite direction. A head-on collision with an oncoming car was only avoided by the skilful driving of the other motorist and the incident was witnessed by a police officer. Upon being questioned Miss Davidson gave a dubious excuse saying that the sun was shining in her eyes and blinded her. As she was travelling away from the rising sun, Superintendent Spratt stated that if her excuse was true 'then Amble is a queer place!'[61] Miss Davidson, who was not present at court, was unsurprisingly found guilty and fined the sum of 15 shillings.

The next case was, again, one of driving without due care. This time the incident had taken place just up the coast at Warkworth. Alnmouth farmer James Frater was charged with an offence that had taken place on the bridge in the village when on the evening of 6 March it was claimed he had collided with a bus. The bridge was a well-known danger spot as it has an arched tower at the southern end and an incline which made visibility difficult; it is also narrow. On the date in question Mr Frater had been driving at approximately 25 mph when the bus was approaching the bridge from the south. Although Superintendent Spratt admitted that it was doubtful Mr Frater could have seen the bus as it passed through the archway he would certainly have been aware of it as it began up the incline on the bridge, yet he had not stopped (as was customary) or even slowed. The bus driver, aware of a rapidly approaching vehicle, stopped but Mr Frater's car ploughed into the front of the bus causing extensive damage to both vehicles. Superintendent Spratt was at a loss to explain Mr Frater's negligence and Mr Frater stated that his foot must have slipped onto the accelerator. Spratt said that the car's brakes were in good working order and that Mr Frater was either not paying attention or had approached the bridge at too fast a speed.   Mr Frater contended that he had not been speeding and that he had in fact braked but had been unable to avoid the collision. His defence also added that although the bus was stationery it had only just braked when Mr Frater's car hit it and that the bridge was a very dangerous one and that any negligence on Mr Frater's part had been miniscule. Mr Frater's solicitor (Mr Wade of Alnwick) endeavoured to shift the blame onto HM Office of Works who had made the bridge a scheduled ancient monument meaning that no alterations could be carried out to make the road safer.[62] Mr Frater pleaded guilty and it was claimed that this had saved the cost of calling witnesses from as far afield as Ashington, Morpeth and Whitely Bay.

Mr Wade went on to emphasise his client's previously clean driving record over twelve years and asked the bench to take into account the dangerous nature of the bridge and to show leniency. The bench fined Mr Frater £1 and endorsed his licence.

Many of the motoring prosecutions were a result of the blackout and lighting restrictions with a typical example being that of Amble miner James Coulson, who was fined 10s for having a crudely home-constructed mask on his front headlamp. This lamp had little effect on the light which was being shown and Mr Coulson was duly prosecuted. Yet another victim was Mr William Davis, a cook from Amble, who was fined 16s for having an overly bright front light and no rear light on his cycle.

Domestic blackout laws also saw a rash of prosecutions in the Amble area where the authorities seem to have been particularly vigilant (probably because of the village's exposed location on the coast). A sitting in April heard several such cases, including two in which light from sitting-room fires had been visible through unshuttered windows. Mr Martin F. Grey was fined the sum of 5s for the offence (Mr Grey, a miner, apologised profusely stating that there was no-one in the house at the time and the fire had burnt up unexpectedly) while Mrs Clara Close was fined 4s for a similar offence. The resentment that the enforcement of the blackout regulations could have was highlighted by the next case. War Reserve police officer Jordan was alerted to an unscreened house light at 5 Smith Street, Amble, on the night of 31 March but could get no answer at the property. He returned at 10.25 pm with PC Henderson and informed the resident, Mr Joseph William Walker, that he would be prosecuted for the offence. Mr Walker responded aggressively telling Jordan and Henderson to 'Get on with the [expletive] job, I'll pay the fine'. As they were leaving he shouted at them saying 'It's a pity you have nothing else to do'![63]

Throughout June and July the police in Alnwick had been trying to trace the source of a light which had been reported by the RAF as being visible from the air. The matter was viewed with some urgency and many police resources were tied up in the search. However it was the resourcefulness of a PC Ireland which solved the case and in doing so revealed the suspicions which had fallen upon those of German or Austrian descent. PC Ireland had been informed that a light was visible from the upstairs of a certain building which overlooked a butcher's shop run by a woman and her son who were of enemy alien descent. Ireland ascended the neighbouring building and observed the light as he had been informed. He immediately questioned the young man who initially denied the offence but on being taken upstairs admitted that the light was indeed visible. In offering prosecution evidence Superintendent Spratt said that the light was in a yard behind buildings and was concealed from the street so that no passing officer would notice it. The defending solicitor, Mr C.W. Forster, stated that the yard was surrounded by tall buildings and that the defendant had a pot outside for cooking meat. He had endeavoured to cover the yard but it seemed that there was a defect in the roof of which he was not aware. He went on that the light was shaded, that the defendant had made every effort to prevent the light showing and that the man, with his mother, was endeavouring to carry on with the family business after his father had been taken from the town and interned. Superintendent Spratt was clearly harbouring hopes of making an example of failure to obey blackout regulations and urged the bench to consider, in future if not in this particular case, using the powers which they had been granted to imprison such offenders. Indirectly referencing the man's foreign connection Spratt continued saying, 'if there is one person in the county of Northumberland who should see that no lights are visible – and I emphasise this – it is the defendant'.[64] The bench took an extremely serious view of the matter but stopped short of imposing a penal sentence, fining the offender the sum of £5 and warning him that any repeat or indeed any other offence of any kind would see him imprisoned.

With breaches of the regulations not decreasing and the wartime situation worsening there was a notable change in attitudes. By July Northumberland JPs were warning that offences breaching the blackout regulations would in future receive far harsher sentences with substantial fines and even imprisonment being likely. At the start of the month Lord Armstrong, sitting at Rothbury, warned that he would be much harsher in future cases. By the middle of the month the Justices on the Amble bench had hardened their stance on blackout violations and handed down their first prison sentences for such offences. The magistrates gave due warning when they imprisoned two Amble miners for one day apiece and fined them both the sum of 10s. The bench commented that they had been urged by the government to crack down on such offences and that 'they would be quite in order' imposing terms of up to three months' imprisonment. They did not wish to take such a drastic step in these cases but would 'make a commencement with to-day with imprisonment and in cases in the future we shall deal with them by imprisonment'. The bench went on to state that the one-day sentences handed down were 'not to be taken as a precedent as to what will come in future. We shall look on these cases with great seriousness indeed. It might be that one light might bring a raider, and there might be no end to the damage that might be done.'[65]

Over-exuberance, exacerbated by the wartime risks that some were facing, could also lead men (and women) into the dock. Two merchant seamen from Amble (both firemen) found themselves charged with being drunk and disorderly on Queen Street. Reserve Sergeant Weallans had observed John William Hewitt and George Robert Stewart acting in a very drunken manner. The two had their arms around each other, were dancing, jostling passers-by, and at one point forced a motorcyclist to swerve violently to avoid them. Weallans was unable to leave the police station at that point but noticed that the two men quietened down after a young man spoke to them to warn them of an approaching constable. However, the two were recognised, duly found guilty and, because there had been several complaints about their behaviour, fined £2 apiece.

With the added stresses of wartime, a relaxing drink, when it was available and for those who could afford it, was one of the few pleasures left and publicans who sought to defraud customers seldom found any sympathy. In early June Mrs Edith Gallon of the Anchor Inn, Wooler, was summonsed for serving under-strength gin and misrepresenting the product. An inspector of weights and measures had ordered a half glass of gin on a visit and been served from a bottle of Gordon's Special London Gin which upon testing had been revealed to be 34.8 under proof. Upon questioning Mr Gallon, who had served him, he was told that it was bulk gin which had been emptied into the bottle from a jar which the drayman was collecting; there was, it was claimed, no intention to sell the gin as Gordon's and the bottle was used because it was the only one available at the time. However, it was admitted that Gordon's was sold at 2d more than bulk gin and Mrs Gallon was subsequently fined two guineas (£2 2s).

The raft of offences which fell under the new acts imposed on wartime Britain resulted in many otherwise law-abiding citizens becoming criminalised and falling afoul of the law. A classic example of this occurred when a North Gosforth vicar, Cecil Gault, was brought before the bench at Alnwick charged with having photographed a small Northumberland harbour without permission. The vicar was approached by a member of the local Home Guard who identified himself and asked for the vicar to produce his identification card. He then informed the vicar that taking photographs of harbour facilities was illegal without written permission but the vicar answered that he had no knowledge of this offence and that there were no signs prohibiting photography (a female companion, however, admitted that she had heard of such a law). The vicar promptly gave up the film which when developed showed the harbour and also two photographs of nearby historical castles. Superintendent Spratt stated that there had been many notices in the press stating what was now illegal and that ignorance was no defence. The defendant continued to argue that he had no knowledge of such a restriction and claimed that he had photographed the location as a beauty spot and believed it to be a 'quiet, derelict fishing village' and 'not of obvious importance'. The bench, however, sided with Superintendent Spratt and fined the vicar £2 12s.[66]

Agriculture

Despite its title as county town, Alnwick's economy was still largely dominated by rural and agricultural affairs with the cattle market being of great importance to the town. In January the government notified the council that it would be taking over the running of the slaughterhouse with the Ministry of Food paying a specified fee per head of cattle passing through; in addition to this the Ministry of Food also planned to buy up all fat stock at Alnwick Cattle Mart.

With the growing importance of securing the national food supply in the face of ongoing submarine and anti-shipping warfare in the Atlantic and on the East Coast, the government and local authorities were keen to make sure that the Northumberland agricultural sector increased its productivity and maintained the morale of its workforce. In early June agricultural labourers received the welcome news that their wages were to be increased to a minimum of 48s per week. The move was enthusiastically backed by the Northumberland Farmer's

Union and the union leaders stated that they were determined to make the policy a success by increasing production for the national effort.

As the year continued the business of auction marts around the county continued with the well-known Rothbury-based firm of Robert Donkin Ltd holding a cash sale of 7,500 lambs at Rothbury in mid-September.

Given the need to grow far more food within Britain, it is no surprise that the government revived an idea from the First World War: the Women's Land Army (WLA). While recruitment began in the summer of 1939, local organisation sometimes took longer and feelings about these new agricultural workers were mixed with many rural organisations being distrustful of what they viewed as unqualified interlopers. Indeed, the National Union of Agricultural Workers reacted to the new organisation with unconcealed venom saying in its magazine, 'The Hon. Mrs This, Lady That and the Countess of Something Else are all on the warpath again. The Women's Land Army is here, and they have all got their old jobs back – of bossing people, and of seeing that the farmers find a way out of their labour shortage without having to pay better wages.'[67]

This attitude displays the class resentment which was commonplace amongst rural communities and the distrust that existed between the farm workers and their employers. However it is important to point out that this was not a view held by all in Northumberland and that, although distrust of the landed classes did indeed run deep within many rural Northumbrian communities, the county had a long history of employing female labour on farms and, by and large, the new volunteers were often more warmly welcomed in the county than elsewhere.[68]

There was no shortage of volunteers coming forward and the biggest problem throughout 1940 remained how to house the young women. Many of the farms and cottages within the county were considered unsuitable but in the Wooler district the WLA and the Young Women's Christian Association (YWCA) cooperated to begin a system of hostels which could house the women.

Using already established and respected members of the local farming community helped the WLA in Northumberland. For example, the appointment of Mr W. Smith of Ryebank, Wooler, helped to ensure that the local branch of the WLA was well organised and had, at its head, someone who was respected by many local farmers. Mr Smith quickly found a suitable hostel for the current volunteers which was large enough to cope with the expected influx of new volunteers by taking over a property at Haugh Head in Wooler.

The chairman of the Northumberland War Ag, Major J.G.G. Rea, was keen to highlight the contribution already being made by the WLA in the county. As early as April he was able to address a meeting stating that the WLA 'had done much to relieve the shortage [of labour] … and some of them had done very good work, even although many of them had never worked before'. Another local landowner, Rotarian J.W. Carmichael, JP, demonstrated the ambiguity of feeling over the work of the WLA in his reply when he criticised the training period allotted to the young women saying that four weeks was nowhere enough time to train them adequately and that, indeed, the training of an 'expert in the industry' took years. Carmichael was somewhat missing the point as it was never intended that the young volunteers of the WLA would be experts in agriculture. He was, however, forced to admit that 'the work done by the WLA had been very valuable and he commended the proposed hostel scheme'.[69]

As the second wartime Christmas approached there was an air of determination mixed with some apprehension. Although the Battle of Britain was seen (and was being portrayed) as being the first great victory of the war, the rest of the military outlook was bleak indeed. Although the evacuation of much of the BEF was heralded as a success it was, as the Prime Minister had stated, not to be given the gloss of a victory. The inhabitants of Northumberland were well aware that Nazi forces were just across the Channel and that they had conquered the majority of Western Europe and Scandinavia. The first casualties from enemy bombing had revealed that the risks were not as great as many pre-war experts had considered, but were also evidence that in this war the civilian was on the front line. Naval losses were also mounting and many in the county worried about the food supply and the increasingly strict rationing of food and other materials.

The scarcity of food drove some to criminal activities. Although cases of outright hoarding were relatively rare in Northumberland there were those who made substantial use of the black market. Although this was illegal and in some cases could be immoral, the majority of such criminal activity was in the form of provisioners providing 'extras' to customers. Others found illicit food supplies in more traditional ways.

The River Coquet at Rothbury had been a traditional haunt of smugglers in the nineteenth century and this tradition was revived by some who were short of food or sensed an opportunity for profit. In November Mr John Shell of Pine Tree House, Rothbury, was arrested for using a gaff to illegally fish for salmon at Thrum Mill, Rothbury. Mr Shell was apprehended by a water bailiff after he was observed gaffing and killing a salmon. Upon arrest Mr Shell had thrown his walking stick and attached gaff into the river in an effort to dispose of some of the evidence but had admitted gaffing the fish. The bailiffs later recovered the gaff and Mr Shell had little option but to plead guilty to the charges against him. While trying to explain his actions Mr Shell stated that his wife liked the taste of salmon and that he acted only to obtain food as rations were 'very scarce just now [but there were] any amount of fish so I thought I would have a bit of fish. I thought there was no harm in having a bit of fish when so many were going past.' The bench was unimpressed by this excuse and fined Mr Shell the sum of £1 2s 6d.

Despite this, morale remained high and the majority of Northumbrians believed that Britain would, in the end, be victorious. The festive period was one in which people tried to recreate something of the happiness of peacetime Christmases but rationing made it difficult for many. For those who were in the armed forces (and those who had family members serving) there was the additional difficulty of separation and uncertainty. In many Northumbrian towns and villages, communities set up huts and other services for the use of locally based soldiers, sailors and airmen.

Berwick was typical of this trend. Early in the war the border community had set up the Berwick Services' Recreation Club and the club convenors were determined to make a special effort for Christmas. Since early in December they had been busily preparing for the Christmas and New Year celebrations and had been eagerly collecting presents, funds and decorations (the centrepiece of which was a Christmas tree complete with coloured electric lights). Much of the funding was secured by the convenors and volunteer staff themselves. The ladies who worked at the club agreed to put aside 2d each for every shift they worked and in such a manner a fine sum was collected in time for the holiday season.

On Christmas Eve the surprised soldiers who attended the club were treated to presents of chocolates and cigarettes and were then given a free concert which included a number of well-known local entertainers. The gift-giving and concerts were continued on every night from Christmas Eve to New Year's Day and gifts were varied (sweets, fruit, etc) with Saturday nights seeing them consisting of boot polish (an item which was greatly welcomed by the recipients). The soldiers were also treated to trifles, jellies and sweets and a special 'Scottish Night' was held to much acclaim (the dancers being especially popular) with many of the soldiers repeatedly thanking the convenors and volunteers.

Despite these attempts at festivity the local newspapers continued (as they had in the previous war) to publish regular lists of casualties. In December, four members of the King's Own Scottish Borderers with local connections were named as having died of wounds, while six Northumberland Fusiliers were listed as being prisoners of war. Such news continued as a constant reminder to those on the home front of the ongoing fighting. Two other Northumberland Fusiliers wrote home from their PoW camps to let their families know that they were well. All three attempted to maintain a cheerful outlook in order to reassure their worried relatives. Fusilier William Coxon of Whittingham wrote to his parents from Stalag IX on 12 October to let them know he was 'quite happy but hope to be with you soon' and urged them not to worry. Fusilier Coxon also asked them to send letters, underclothes, socks, tobacco and food parcels if possible. His comrade, Fusilier Ronnie Henry, wrote to his parents in Tweedmouth that he had 'a comfortable billet and a clean bed' and that the work that the Germans had put him to (on local farms) was alright. He also urged them not to worry, asked how things were with them, and expressed concern that he hadn't heard from them for some time.

Another Northumbrian prisoner of war to write home at around this time was Gunner Billie Carr of Alnwick. Billie wrote home to his parents (he was an only son) at 7 Howick Street to let them know that he was well and that 'little Billie is getting a big boy' (presumably little Billie was his son). Gunner Carr also expressed the hope that he would be home soon and urged his parents and other family not to worry.[70]

Battle of Britain
On 15 August the north east came under attack from the only massed

raid that took place over the area during the Battle of Britain. The Luftwaffe, believing that all of Fighter Command's front line squadrons were in the south of the country and that the north was practically undefended, launched a force from the Norway-based Luftflotte 5 to stretch the defences while an attack on the south would take place simultaneously.

The attacks on the south came first. These largely concentrated on airfields and were designed to keep the attention of Fighter Command focused firmly on the south of England. However, fate played a role and, unbeknownst to the Luftwaffe, the radar operators of 13 Group were on full alert monitoring for possible attacks on a large convoy expected to sail from Hull. Just after midday they detected a raid which at first was believed to be heading for Edinburgh. As it became clear that the raid was stronger than at first believed and was altering course southwards the decision was taken to scramble the Spitfires of 72 Squadron from Acklington with orders to head for the Farnes while 79 Squadron's Hurricanes were placed on standby. Subsequently the Hurricanes of 605 and 607 Squadrons were also placed on standby.

As the radar picture became clearer it was obvious that this was a serious raid. The more northerly of the two German formations was in fact a diversion intended to draw off fighters and consisted of HE 115 seaplanes which had orders to turn back before reaching the coast. Unfortunately any chance of the deception working was destroyed as the lead navigator of the actual bombing force, which consisted of 72 HE 111s led by Oberstleutnant Fuchs, had made an error and was too far north meaning that the radar return seen by 13 Group seemed to be one very large raid and Air Vice-Marshal (AVM) Saul reacted appropriately. The operators were also aware of a more southerly and smaller plot which was in fact the escort which had been assigned to Fuchs' formation. This escort consisted of twenty-one long range ME 110s loaded with extra fuel and led by their commander, Werner Restemeyer. Upon sighting the two formations attempting to link up, 72 Squadron reported a raid of 100 plus enemy aircraft with the result that three further squadrons were scrambled (41, 607, which was ordered to patrol Tyneside, and 79).

Meanwhile 72 Squadron found itself in an ideal position to attack, being some 4,000 feet higher than the German formations. Squadron Leader Edward (Ted) Graham was at first slightly nonplussed as to what action was best and when asked by another pilot if he had seen the Germans stammered the now infamous reply, 'Of course I've seen the b-b-b-bastards, I'm t-t-t-trying to work out what to do,' before leading his squadron down in a flank attack on the escorts which took them through into the bomber formation below.[71] Two ME 110s were immediately shot down, including Restemeyer's which blew up dramatically when bullets hit the fuel tank, and the escorts scattered in confusion. The subsequent attack on the bombers also resulted in the formation losing coherency and many of the Heinkels jettisoned their bombs in panic. Five minutes later RAF reinforcements arrived and very quickly a further eight HE 111s and six more ME 110s were shot down for only two damaged Hurricanes (both from 605 Squadron) and one wounded pilot.

AVM Richard E. Saul CB DFC had handled his forces in an exemplary manner and they, along with the Tyne anti-aircraft defences, had turned aside a major Luftwaffe attack for no serious loss to themselves and with little or no damage done on the ground. The action was witnessed by few people directly although many Northumbrians in coastal towns and villages saw aircraft and heard the combats, and at Amble four German airmen were brought ashore after their HE 111 had been shot down off Druridge Bay. The actions of the RAF aircrew and the tactics of AVM Saul resulted in the Luftwaffe giving up any hope of launching further heavy daylight raids on Northumberland and Tyneside.[72]

Air Vice Marshall Saul was a skilled commander with authority over Northern England and Scotland (Public Domain).

The local press reported the event with a substantial dose of hyperbole claiming that the enemy force had consisted of over 300 aircraft and that their 'wings darkened the sky over the North Sea'. They claimed that the RAF had managed to shoot down '75 bombers in as many minutes without loss to themselves'.[73]

CHAPTER THREE

1941

Struggling On

Although the majority of bombing had fallen on London and the south east, the people of the ARP and medical services in Northumberland continued to play their part. Two Berwickshire members of the St. John Ambulance Brigade (Mrs Campbell of Tweedsmouth and Miss L. McConville of Tintagel House, Berwick) returned from a two-week period of service in the capital on 6 January. During this period the two nurses worked in underground shelters through several raids including one of the heaviest of the blitz when thousands of incendiary bombs were dropped on the capital. The two were keen to discuss their experiences and to pass on what they had learned to the local ARP and emergency services.

News of the courage under fire of a Berwick man emerged at the beginning of January when it was announced that a bar had been added to the MC of Captain David C. McCreath of the 1st (East African) Light Battery. The award was for extreme courage during the Battle of Tug Argan in British Somaliland when Captain McCreath had directed the fire of his battery despite his observation post having been destroyed. Exposed to enemy artillery and small arms fire, Captain McCreath continued to direct fire for two days until his battery was knocked out. Even then McCreath had joined the infantry and helped to direct their mortar fire from an exposed position. The citation

*Captain David McCreath, awarded the MC for bravery in Africa (*Berwickshire News*).*

stated that he did so with 'complete disregard to his own safety' and 'inspired courage in others by his utter contempt of danger'.[74] Surrounded and outnumbered by the Italian forces, Captain McCreath was at first posted missing before it was revealed that he had in fact been taken prisoner.

Captain McCreath came from a well-known Berwickshire family with properties at both Berwick and Norham and had married into an equally well-known family in 1936 (his bride was Miss Jean Burnside Wight). An experienced officer, Captain McCreath had earned his first MC in the First World War as a member of the Royal Artillery and had subsequently served with the 7th (Territorial) Battalion, Northumberland Fusiliers, before moving to Kenya in 1926 where he became a coffee planter. At the outbreak of the war he joined the King's African Rifles but then transferred to the 1st (East African) Light Battery.

Despite the grim war news a happy event resulted in comment in the national papers towards the end of January when Mrs Carr-Ellison of The Rectory at Howick gave birth to triplet daughters. As unusual as this event was in itself the fact that caused amused talk was that Mrs Carr-Ellison's mother had given birth to twin daughters and her grandmother to a single daughter. Where would it end, speculated the *Daily Mirror*? Would the next generation of Carr-Ellison's bring quadruplet daughters?

In 1941 the authorities continued to react with harshness when confronted with cases of people ignoring or breaching the blackout laws. Three cases heard at Rothbury at the beginning of the year were typical of these offences. Two involved the same property, Brackenrigg Cottage, Rothbury. The first offence took place on the night of 23 November when PC Davenport reported seeing a very bright unscreened light shining from a double window but that when he knocked on the door there was no answer and he was informed that the resident, Joseph William

*Mrs Carr-Ellison, whose triplets caused amused comment in the national press (*Daily Mirror*)*

Cottice, had returned to his home in Sunderland. PC Davenport was left with no choice but to break the window in order to enter the cottage and turn off the light. Mr Cottice wrote to the bench to tell them that he had no idea who had left the light on but he accepted that it was his responsibility. He was fined £1.

The second case took place on the evening of 15 December when Reserve Sergeant Carruthers reported seeing a bright light from a window of the same cottage but once again there was no-one at home when he attempted to gain entry. Sergeant Carruthers later saw the resident, Mr Septimus Marshall of Westcliffe, Pondicherry, Rothbury, and was told that the light must have been left on accidentally. Mr Marshall, a ship owner, was fined the same sum of £1 for the offence.

The third case illustrated that the blackout laws ran throughout the hours of darkness, not just at nightfall. The accused, Mrs Elizabeth Redhead of the Market Place, was charged with having shown an unscreened light from an upstairs window of her home at 8.10 on the morning of 10 December 1940. It seems that Mrs Redhead had gone into the room with a candle to get clothing from a wardrobe and had not noticed that the blackout blind had been taken down; she claimed that it was quite light at the time, a defence which was not helped by the fact that she had needed a candle. The bench was unimpressed and told Mrs Redhead that there was just as much risk of aerial attack in the early morning as at night and fined her 10s.

In April a serious case of wounding came before the bench at Rothbury. Fifty-year-old Miss Isobel Jane Selby Dixon of Gate Cottage, Garleigh Road, Rothbury, was accused of wounding her long-time friend Miss Jane Anne Soulsby (75) at Central Buildings, Rothbury on the night of 22 March. It would seem that the trouble between the two friends (Miss Dixon visited Miss Soulsby on an almost daily basis) had begun at the start of the year when Miss Soulsby noticed that some money had gone missing from her house at a time when Miss Dixon was her only visitor. She had asked Dixon about it but she had denied any knowledge of the money and Soulsby later mentioned this matter to the relieving officer. On the night of Saturday, 22 March, there was a knock on Miss Soulsby's door and, upon answering, the defendant had entered the property and sat down with her hand in her coat pocket. The police officer giving evidence stated that Miss Soulsby was an elderly woman but was of sound mind and that her memory was reliable. It was alleged that Miss Dixon then accused her former friend of telling the relieving officer that she had taken money from her. She stood up, produced a bottle from her pocket, and began striking Miss Soulsby on the head so ferociously that the bottle broke and Miss Soulsby fell to the floor bleeding from head wounds. It would appear that at that point Dixon fled and after some time Soulsby managed to rouse herself and wash the blood off as best she could before alerting a neighbour who fetched a doctor and the police. After treatment, the police ascertained the story from Soulsby and spoke to Dixon who claimed that she had never left the house that night.

Giving evidence, Miss Soulsby confirmed that the two had been friends for a long time and that Dixon frequently came over to the house for her tea or supper (Miss Soulsby concluded that she had perhaps been 'too good' to Miss Dixon) but that at the start of the year she had left the defendant alone in her house peeling potatoes while she went on a message for half an hour. Later that night Miss Soulsby had noticed that £17 had gone missing. Miss Soulsby said this was 'a big loss for me' and she had asked Miss Dixon about the money several times but the defendant had always denied any knowledge of the matter. Miss Soulsby claimed that on the night of the attack she had been about to go to bed when she went to the door and Miss Dixon walked in. She stated, 'I said I was sorry I had no supper for her. She asked if I had seen the relieving officer. Then she was into my head with the bottle, and I thought I was a gonner [sic]. Another blow would have finished me.' Miss Soulsby claimed she did not know how many times she was struck but that she fell to the ground and that Dixon had 'walked out, never looking behind or speaking. I said "Oh Selby Dixon".'

Miss Soulsby claimed that she had worked on cleaning her wounds all night without sleeping until 8 am the next morning when she alerted her neighbour and asked her to get a nurse and doctor. Under cross-examination Miss Soulsby testified that the accused knew that she had the £17 (which she had saved from selling teas at the Jubilee Hall before the war) and she had 'been poaching about'. She also confirmed that despite poor eyesight she was certain in her identification of the accused. Several neighbours testified that they had seen Miss Dixon visiting regularly with an upstairs neighbour reporting that she had heard the sound of a thump, like someone falling at the time. Another,

Miss Jane Parsons, said that when summonsed by Miss Soulsby on the Sunday morning she found Miss Soulsby in a 'terrible state ... her clothing ... saturated with blood', but clear-headed and that she had sent for medical attention before summoning the police at the urging of the doctor.

Given that the defendant had claimed not to have left her house on the night in question the testimony of local bus driver, George Edward Diery, was particularly damning. Mr Diery, of Wagtail Road, stated that he had known both women for many years and that on the night in question he had been crossing the bridge into the village when he noticed Miss Dixon walking towards him from Bridge Street and that she had crossed the road to avoid him but that when he looked back she had crossed back again.

Doctor A.S. Hedley testified that he had been summoned to attend to Miss Soulsby and found her remarkably clear headed with little sign of concussion (although this was over twelve hours after the attack) and upon examination he found two lacerations on her scalp. She also complained of pain in her jaw. The doctor stated that it was very clear that Miss Soulsby had lost a lot of blood.

Superintendent Cruikshank stated that he had observed the broken and bloodstained bottle (which he produced as evidence) at the property of Miss Soulsby and that he had visited Miss Dixon who had denied the assault and claimed to have not left the house after 7.30 pm on the night in question. The officer arrested her and took her to the police station where he noticed that the gloves she wore bore a noticeable stain; the police sent the gloves to be analysed at the Home Office Laboratory which concluded that there were two stains and both were human blood.

Giving her evidence, the defendant claimed that Miss Soulsby had accused her of taking $2 (she sometimes got Canadian money sent to her by a relative) and that she had said she 'would have to see about that, because she could not have Miss Soulsby spoiling her good character'.[75] She also repeated her claim to have not left the house and claimed that two ladies known to her had visited and left at around dusk after which she went to bed. Miss Dixon claimed to have been working in her garden and said the blood on her gloves was a result of her cutting herself on a gooseberry bush. When under cross-examination she vehemently denied striking Miss Soulsby.

Miss Dixon's legal counsel attempted to sway the jury by claiming that much of the evidence could be mistaken (he alleged that mistakes like this had been made in the recent past), that some was contradictory and that Mr Diery could have been mistaken about the date or the identity of the woman he had seen (even though Mr Diery had denied both these suggestions under cross-examination). He also said that if this was a capital case the jury would not convict and that Miss Dixon had lived in Rothbury for fifty years with a spotless character and reiterated that if there was any doubt the benefit should be given to Miss Dixon.

The bench retired to consider the evidence which had been put before them and upon their return the chairman (Lord Armstrong) stated that they were convinced of the guilt of Miss Dixon and that they were sentencing her to prison for a period of three months.

Juvenile crime and acts committed by younger members of the community were of particular concern. Many children were in increased danger of becoming criminalised due to lack of parental guidance (parents were often away in the forces or working longer hours) and the restrictions in school hours. A special court held at Rothbury in May heard a case of theft which involved juveniles, women and members of the services. The alleged crime involved the theft of several minor household items from a caravan at Pauperhaugh on two separate occasions in April. The accused were a serving soldier, Reuben Vincent Lee, who seems to have exploited the affections of 18-year-old domestic servant Edith Caroline McKay of Brinkburn; the other accused was an unnamed 15-year-old girl. McKay was also charged with having stolen a £1 note from her mother's house at Brinkburn. Giving evidence, Miss McKay stated that on 17 April she had met Lee, whom she had known for a short time, and the two had gone for a walk along the river but had missed the bus home and that Lee had walked with her as far as Pauperhaugh where he broke into the unoccupied caravan of Mrs Gowans (who lived at Alnwick) and the two remained there until 4 am. When leaving, the two both stole several items including a teapot, a mirror and a piece of velvet cloth. Miss McKay said that Lee had stolen the mirror as he wanted it for shaving while he took the cloth for polishing his boots (he also stole a cup); she took the teapot and a pair of sandshoes. Two or three days later Miss McKay had persuaded the 15-year-old to accompany her to the caravan to get some items (mainly consisting of crockery and tableware) for her mother and said she had warned the girl not to tell her mother where they had come from. She told her mother that she had obtained the items from a fictitious Mrs Brodie. Miss McKay further admitted taking the £1 note and used it to buy a pair of shoes, stockings and a bus ticket to a dance held at Longframlington. She used the remainder to take a bus to Ashington where she stayed for the weekend, attending another dance, and spending most of Monday at Morpeth. Miss McKay declared that she had been led astray by her 'liking for the company of boys' and concluded that she 'would like to be sent to a home'. In his evidence Lee corroborated the story of the missed bus adding that he and Miss McKay had remained on Pauperhaugh Bridge talking for two hours but had sought shelter from the rain in the caravan. However he claimed that McKay had told him the caravan had not been used for two years and that her father was an officer in the RAF and the family had owned an MG car which the Army had taken over at the start of the war. Lee admitted breaking in and taking the items but said that it was only because he believed the woman's story and believed the caravan to be disused. He had never been in trouble before (a fact confirmed by the police) and his officer testified to his excellent character adding that Lee was entrusted with 'hundreds of pounds of equipment, handled the rations, and was very trustworthy'.[76] The bench concluded that the ringleader of the whole affair was indeed Miss McKay and ordered that she be put on probation for two years with the condition that she spend one year at a home in Newcastle. Lee was bound over to the sum of £5 for a year while the 15-year-old girl had her charges adjourned *sine die* (indefinitely); she was informed that the probation officer would be keeping an eye on her and that the slightest relapse into crime would see the charges reinstated immediately.

There were a number of cases of theft in rural areas during the period with many of them involving the theft of foodstuffs and other essential supplies. In June a Gosforth man and a 14-year-old boy were found guilty of the theft, on two occasions, of seventy-six eggs from hen houses at Brinkburn (the properties of Captain L. Fenwick and Mr Edward Cuthbert). The two, who were driving a delivery lorry, were stopped by the police and confessed to the thefts; the driver, William Rutter Rutherford, claimed he wanted the eggs for his mother. The bench took an extremely dim view of the crime stating that the two 'should realise the seriousness of this charge ... Food today is altogether a different thing from what it was before the war.' Mr Rutherford was fined the sum of £2 5s and the boy was placed on probation for a year with the stern warning that he must mend his ways or he 'would only end up in a bad career', but that if he took the chance offered to him 'he might become a credit to himself and his country'.[77]

Other crimes were more minor in nature but still aroused deep anger in official circles. The blackout gave increased opportunities for crimes such as burglary, robbery and petty theft, and it would seem that the public conveniences at Wooler were a repeated target. On 14 December the doors had been broken open and the lock, which held the money which people paid to enter, stolen. Although the theft was thought to have amounted to no more than three or four shillings, this was the third or fourth time this had occurred within a month and the police had been unable to trace those responsible despite keeping a watch during the hours of darkness.

While the Battle of Britain had ended in victory (or at least a stalemate which favoured Britain) the German bombing campaign continued as the war entered its third year. Although north Northumberland was not a prime target, it did receive its share of bombs and mines which sometimes resulted in casualties. Even isolated spots could attract the attentions of the Luftwaffe, especially if there happened to be some sort of military installation nearby. On the night of 23/24 February the Germans attacked several north-east towns. Davidson's Farm at Longhorsley attracted four bombs which were probably aimed at a nearby searchlight battery; thankfully there were no casualties. The only damage reported was to the farmhouse at Townhead Farm.

A month later, the Luftwaffe returned to raid the industries of Tyneside while other aircraft scattered bombs over Northumberland. Seemingly lost and making landfall to the north of its intended target one bomber dropped several bombs in the Berwick area. These included 100 incendiary bombs at Scremerston Town Farm and six high explosive bombs at Cheswick Buildings Farm; neither caused any significant damage. Days later a small number of aircraft mounted surprise attacks over Northumberland with one targeting the LNER main line at Littlehoughton and another the pipe works at

Longhoughton. The most serious incident was when a Luftwaffe bomber flew low over Alnwick before machine-gunning troops at Embleton and a goods train. One of the bombs which had been aimed at the rail line failed to explode and caused some disruption until it was made safe later in the day.

The night of 13/14 March once again saw the Luftwaffe mount attacks on a variety of northern towns and cities. At RAF Acklington the anti-aircraft batteries attempted to bring down several aircraft which passed over but it was a 72 Squadron Spitfire from the airfield which scored the only success of the night when Flight Lieutenant D. Sheen attacked a Junkers JU88. The Luftwaffe aircraft was observed going down in flames off the coast at Amble and the body of Oberleutnant H. Voigtländer-Tetzner was found at sea.

Raids continued throughout March with lone bombers sometimes dropping bombs or mines at seemingly random locations in north Northumberland. Although little damage was done, that which did occur often caused considerable inconvenience. Just after 8 pm on 26 March a single raider dropped two parachute mines near Felton; although there were no casualties, the mines damaged electricity cables. The attacks continued into April with the afternoon of the 1st seeing bombs dropped at Christon Bank and that night the LNER line was again a target with traffic being machine-gunned by enemy aircraft near Berwick.

On the night of 7 April enemy bombers once again scattered bombs over a wide range of north Northumberland communities. Shortly before midnight the Wooler district found itself under attack with approximately thirty bombs and hundreds of incendiary bombs being dropped in the area. Thankfully the bombing caused no casualties and only slight damage to properties. Other areas which experienced bombs included a field near the Rothbury to Forestburn Gate road where two parachute mines fell, Alwinton, Lilburn, Callaly and Ford; once again there were no casualties and damage was slight.

Although the raids had so far caused little damage there is no doubt that they were affecting the lives of the people of north Northumberland. For many residents it had become routine to have a night's sleep disturbed by the wail of air raid sirens and, for some, to hear the worrying whistle and explosion of bombs. Hitting back at the raiders was extremely difficult. Although Northumbrians liked to hear the anti-aircraft batteries firing, most of the rare successes came from the aircraft of RAF Fighter Command which were stationed in the county. On the evening of 10 April a lone Junkers JU88 on a reconnaissance of Newcastle fell victim to two Spitfires over Alnmouth; again, the Spitfires were from 72 Squadron.[78]

A daylight raid by a single JU88 on 28 April did cause casualties. The target was the 310 Coastal Defence Battery of the Royal Artillery at Spittal. Of the four bombs dropped two fell into the sea and two in the town. One of these smashed through four gas tanks at the North of England Chemical Works before exploding in the mill of the firm Johnson & Darling Ltd. Sixteen people were injured, one of them seriously, with the injured initially being treated at the local first aid post before nine of the more seriously injured were transferred to Berwick Infirmary. Damage was quite extensive with the chemical works and two manure works (Johnson & Darling Ltd and J.J Cunningham's) being temporarily put out of action, and in the town ninety-eight properties were damaged to varying degrees.

The most serious injury resulting from the raid was ARP Warden Richard Hankinson who was buried by debris and badly injured. Many of the injuries in the town were to housewives who had been cut by flying glass after the windows of their homes had been blown in. Others to suffer included a bedridden woman named Burns who lived with her married daughter Mrs Dixon; their house was badly damaged by blast and rendered uninhabitable. Particularly unfortunate were Mr James Grey and his family who had moved to Berwick (he was a native of the town). After being bombed out of their homes in the south of England, they were forced to evacuate their home in Berwick after it too was badly damaged. James had served in the Royal Navy during the First World War.[79]

There were stories of determination and courage during the raid. A Mrs Ford, who lived very close to where one of the bombs exploded, was widely praised for possibly saving the lives of several children. Mrs Ford and the children had been standing outside her house when the JU88 appeared. She realised it was a German when it began machine-gunning the coastal battery. Thinking quickly, Mrs Ford ushered the children inside and, closing her door, told them to take cover. The ARP services said that it was her quick thinking which saved the children from serious injury or worse.

Throughout the raid the ARP services, police and ambulance personnel acted with calm determination and the townspeople too recovered from the initial shock very quickly to help those who had been bombed out. Very soon after the raid repair squads from Berwick and neighbouring towns went into action to repair properties which could be made habitable once more.

One small boy also showed a stoic and calm demeanour towards the devastation caused by the raid when he picked his way through the wreckage and went into a barber's shop to ask for a haircut. The barber was unable to fulfil this wish as his premises had been damaged but said to the lad, also showing considerable spirit, 'Call to-morrow, Sonny'.[80]

With the restrictions on petrol and the demands of living in a largely rural area with difficult terrain it is no wonder that many of the local authorities in north Northumberland found holding regular meetings problematic. In early June, Rothbury Rural District Council agreed to change their schedule from monthly to quarterly meetings with the lack of petrol and the exigencies of farming being cited as the prime reasons. In order to maintain orderly running of the council this meant placing more decisions in the hands of the War Emergency Committee (consisting of Mr N. Snaith, Mr John Snaith, Mr F.R. Ord and Mr Clark) and authorising the Finance Committee to spend up to £100 in emergencies without calling a full meeting of the council. This convinced one member of the council, Mr T. Carruthers, to withdraw his resignation as this had been due to his being unable to attend the monthly meetings as often as he wished.

The men and women who served as air raid wardens, manned first aid posts and volunteered to serve in rescue squads in Northumberland were from hugely varied backgrounds and every level of society. Their efforts during the air raids of 1941 attracted widespread praise from both the authorities and the local population, although there was criticism when wardens were seen as being pernickety or exceeding their authority. Although north Northumberland did not attract particularly heavy raiding, these volunteers were often exposed to danger when they did occur and were also often required to lend aid to neighbouring areas, especially during the heavy raids on Tyneside during 1941.

The largely rural character of the majority of north Northumberland presented its own difficulties when it came to the dangers of bombing. Although unlikely to be targeted directly it had already become clear that German bombers would and did attack targets of opportunity when the chance arose. The danger presented to isolated farming communities by incendiary bombs was a key area of concern as entire stocks of valuable agricultural produce could easily be destroyed before the scattered fire services could respond. It was decided early in the year that a system of volunteer fire watchers be established in rural areas. A meeting of Rothbury Rural Council held in February heard that Rothbury had been divided into thirty-one groups, that volunteers were being actively recruited and that the village was now very well covered. The meeting also urged small farming hamlets of more than three or four cottages to consider buying their own stirrup pump (at a cost of £1) and sandbags; to prepare for this a supply of sandbags had been stored and twenty-six stirrup pumps ordered.

Despite this there seems to have been a fairly lax attitude in Rothbury as the council surveyor was able to tell a council meeting in June that, although there were many volunteer fire watchers who came out during alerts, it 'was really up to people themselves now to look after their own property'.[81] He also stated that although Rothbury was not in a compulsory area (for fire-watching training) the decision had been taken to distribute stirrup pumps around the area and to train as many fire-watchers as possible in their use.

As we have seen, the pilots of 72 Squadron enjoyed some success against the April raiders but the risks facing the pilots, who were often required to operate over the sea, were made clear when the aircraft of Sergeant Bernard Collyer was lost after attacking a JU88 on 29 April. Sergeant Collyer went into cloud and was last heard saying that his engine had failed and that he was ditching in the North Sea; Collyer's body was found at sea later the same day.[82] The squadron gained some measure of revenge the next day when Sergeants White and Harrison attacked and shot down another JU88 into the sea off the Farne Islands.

On 27 March the residents of Seahouses and nearby coastal villages received a shock when the 6,809-ton SS *Somali* exploded just off Beadnell Point. The SS *Somali* had been attacked the day before off Blyth but was being towed by a tug and escorted by the lifeboats from both Seahouses and Boulmer when it was reported that a fire broke out leading to a colossal explosion which blew out windows in Seahouses.

SS Somali *blowing up off Beadnell Point.*

The lifeboats survived, miraculously, with their crews understandably shaken. It was rumoured that the *Somali* had been carrying explosives, which could perhaps account for the nature of the explosion, while some accounts state that she was torpedoed.

While the majority of losses off the coast of Northumberland were merchant vessels, a rather unusual service ship was lost on the night of 27 April when HMS *Patia* was sunk by an enemy bomber off Seahouses. HMS *Patia* was one of the five Fighter Catapult Ships of the Pegasus Class which were converted from a variety of merchant vessels. The idea was that the ship would accompany a convoy and, if attacked from the air, would launch its aircraft to attack the enemy bombers. The fighter would then ditch and the pilot would be picked up by the convoy. HMS *Patia* was a former ocean boarding vessel which was hurriedly converted on the Tyne and equipped with a catapult and either a Fairey Fulmar or Hurricane aircraft in addition to upgraded anti-aircraft weaponry. Sailing from the Tyne to Belfast on her maiden voyage, HMS *Patia* was attacked by a Heinkel HEIII bomber which came out of low cloud. Although badly hit by a bomb which caused many casualties, the anti-aircraft guns scored a direct hit which caused the bomber to crash into the sea. Unfortunately HMS *Patia* was by this time sinking and the order was given to abandon ship.

Forty of the crew, including the captain (Commander David Marion Burton Baker), were killed when the ship sank and thirty-one survivors, many of them injured by shrapnel, found themselves adrift in lifeboats. Witnessing the sinking from the shore, several local communities launched their lifeboats to search for survivors. The desperate search lasted through the night before all the survivors were rescued and safely brought ashore where they were cared for by local residents until the authorities could take over.[83]

We have seen in the previous chapter how the beaches and hinterland at Druridge Bay were a vulnerable point and a likely landing site for any German invasion or raid. By 1941 the defending troops of the 162nd Infantry had been replaced by men from the newly raised 202nd Independent Infantry Brigade (Home).[84] The men of the 162nd had been stretched thinly and the 202nd, along with the 216th and 225th Brigades (which together formed the Northumberland County Division), had been raised, by the 2nd Infantry Training Group based in Northumberland, specifically for the task of defending the Northumberland coastline. The brigade consisted of the following units: 11th Battalion, King's Regiment (Liverpool) (left November); 12th Battalion, King's Regiment (Liverpool) (left May 1941); 11th Battalion, Green Howards (left November 1941); and 7th Battalion, East Lancashire Regiment (left November 1941). The brigade had a brief life and was disbanded on 1 December 1941 with several of the battalions becoming light anti-aircraft formations or being transferred to other infantry brigades; brief attachment was also served in November by 9th Battalion, Green Howards.

Of course, these units alone were insufficient and the defences, both at Druridge and the rest of Northumberland, were also manned by members of the Home Guard and by units such as the 9th (Northumbrian) Defence Regiment, Royal Artillery, whose 938th Battery manned two 6-pounder guns at Druridge and Hemscott Hill. Other artillery guarding Druridge by 1941 included two 60-pounder guns, a 4.75mm coastal gun to the rear, and a coastal battery at Hemscott Hill with two 6-inch guns and two searchlights manned by 311th Battery, 510th Coast Regiment, Royal Artillery.

As the defences were reorganised throughout 1941 they became concentrated on defensive nodal points as well as the front line beach defences. These nodal points included positions at Druridge itself,

Hemscott Hill and, to the rear, Chibburn. Widdrington and Widdrington Station also got defensive sites consisting of machine gun positions and anti-invasion ditches while the open farmland was protected from aerial landings by trenches and other obstructions. The manning of the coastal defences at Druridge throughout most of 1941 fell to the men of the 7th Battalion, East Lancashire Regiment, which placed one company manning the defences at all times and a further company in reserve towards the rear of the position at Widdrington. The nodal points at Druridge were manned by only a single platoon of men with a further platoon which manned two 6-pounder guns and a searchlight. To house these men a number of accommodation huts were constructed at sites throughout the defended area. At Widdrington the manning of the defences (which largely consisted of pillboxes, sandbagged positions and roadblocks) was the responsibility of 3rd Battalion, Northumberland Home Guard.

Many of the defensive sites at Druridge Bay are still extant and can be seen today. They include the anti-tank blocks, pillboxes, anti-tank ditches and loopholed walls. Two of the pillboxes are particularly

Disguised pillbox at Druridge (© Russel Wills).

noteworthy. For reasons of camouflage one, just off the road approaching Druridge, was built to look like a ruined cottage, while the other was constructed inside the remains of a medieval Order of St. John of Jerusalem preceptor at Chibburn.

At the defended village of Wooler construction of pillboxes continued apace with the area being prepared for an all-round defence against invasion. Roadblocks and at least twelve pillboxes were in place with the defensive responsibilities falling to 1st (Berwick) Battalion, Northumberland Home Guard and the 225th Independent Infantry Brigade (which throughout 1941 had its headquarters in Wooler).[85]

The stop lines which were created and manned throughout the year usually followed geographical features across Northumberland and were designed to delay any invading force and, if necessary, to deny passage southwards. In order to do so every bridge was prepared with explosives and would have been detonated if the position became untenable. The Coquet Stop Line, for example, followed much of the course of the River Coquet and included trenches, pillboxes, roadblocks and other defences. How effective these measures would have been against any organised invasion is, however, debateable.

Throughout the year the government encouraged the residents of Northumberland to back the war effort through charitable causes such as the War Savings Campaign. Slogans such as 'War Savings are Warships' and 'Save your way to Victory' were common in the poster and advertising campaigns which urged people to take part.

*War Savings adverts encouraged Northumbrians to support the war effort (*Morpeth Herald*).*

Other campaigns were both more localised and more direct. The Rothbury War Weapons Campaign held a special fundraising week in July and by the end of it the regional secretary announced that to date the total pledged was over £70,000. The sum raised during the week far outmatched the initial aim of the campaign which was to raise sufficient funds to purchase a bomber (£20,000) and by the end of the week over £32,000 had been raised. The week's events were opened by Lord and Lady Armstrong of Cragside and began with a parade of military units, the local Home Guard, civil defence services, Boy Scouts, Girl Guides and Brownies, accompanied by the North Seaton Colliery Prize Band.

Amongst the more effective propaganda slogans used to encourage the people of Rothbury Rural District to donate were 'Rothbury, Awake – Give Hitler a Shake' and 'Make Money Boom – Send Hitler to his Doom'. The organisers praised the people of the district for the magnificent way in which everyone had rallied around the cause. It was not only the community of Rothbury which supported the week. The hamlets and farmsteads of Elsdon, Longframlington, Lee, Harbottle, Thropton, Whittingham, Netherton and Biddlestone all formed local committees and held events such as whist drives, concerts, dances, fancy dress parades and events specifically for children. To aid

*Advert for Rothbury's War Weapons Week campaign (*Morpeth Herald*).*

in the spread of the message, a mobile cinema van toured the hills of upper Coquetdale showing propaganda films and music.

At Rothbury there were dances and other events with a grand fete held in the grounds of Cragside on the Wednesday. The streets of the village were decorated and there was what was described as a 'cheerfully aggressive spirit'. The gardens and grounds were opened to the public by Lord Armstrong and stalls and games were organised. The week culminated in a children's sports day which also included singing competitions and folk dancing. So successful was the week that it was hoped that by the time the final collections were tallied the fund might be sufficient to purchase two bombers.[86]

The fundraising week had a spin-off at the village of Elsdon when a local committee was formed to organise subsidiary events to raise funds for a memorial for any Elsdonians who might lose their lives in the war, to pay for a public reception of those who had served after victory, and to pay for a new hall.[87]

The area of Berwick and Spittal, as we have seen, was a constant target. It was a coastal town with a harbour and the main LNER line ran through it. In the early hours of August Bank Holiday Monday, a raider dropped two bombs in the main street at Spittal and caused severe damage and casualties. The final toll was six dead, three seriously injured and a further eight with minor injuries. Amongst the serious injuries were Mrs Gladys Wilkie (74) who suffered cuts, bruises and severe shock, Mr Andrew Pattison (27) who suffered a compound fracture of the left leg and head injuries (he was standing across the street from where the bombs hit), and Mrs Cynthia Mercy who suffered severe shock and bruising.

The Whitlie family were at home when their house was struck and collapsed. Trapped in the wreckage were Mr and Mrs John Whitlie, their 12-year-old son Douglas, their young daughter and Mrs Whitlie's parents (Mr John Wilkie and his wife). A rescue squad immediately set to work attempting to extricate the family and quickly came across Mrs Whitlie. While working to rescue her, the trapped woman chatted with her rescuers telling them of her confidence in them and describing how she thought she was trapped. Meanwhile other rescuers had discovered the body of Mr Wilkie huddled over the body of his 12-year-old grandson whom he had obviously been trying to shield from the falling debris. The attempt to rescue Mrs Whitlie went on feverishly for some considerable time and she began asking 'if the others in the house were safe'. The leader of the rescue squad admitted that they 'had not the heart to tell her that her father and little boy were dead'. After Mrs Whitlie was rescued and taken to hospital (she had only minor injuries) the leader of the rescue squad told reporters, 'If ever there was a heroine she is one'. Mr Whitlie and Mrs Wilkie were extricated with minor injuries while the Whitlies' daughter escaped uninjured.

In a neighbouring property Mr and Mrs Henry Wilson were hosting their niece Miss Rita Rollo when their house was hit and all three were killed; Rita had been due to resume her studies the following day. The final fatality of the raid was a Mrs Dixon who was killed in the house where she lived alone.

Two houses were destroyed with a further three having to be subsequently demolished. A hundred houses were damaged, twelve of them seriously enough that they were rendered temporarily uninhabitable. Other properties to be damaged included Allan's Garage (which suffered severe damage), three public houses (including the Red Lion which was severely damaged by blast), Johnstone & Darling's mill (again), J.J. Cunningham's manure factory, and St. Paul's Presbyterian Church. There were post-raid reports of an unexploded bomb at Gibson's Row which caused a mass evacuation but was later disproved.

One of the houses to be demolished belonged to the newly married Mr and Mrs Leslie Sidey. The house was next door to those which were destroyed by the bombs and took the full force of the blast leaving wedding presents, many of which had never been used, scattered in all directions across the street. The damage which resulted led ARP workers to state that 'the town presented a pitiful sight with debris and glass lying everywhere to a considerable depth. Rescue parties reported that household effects were picked up all over the place, and a considerable amount of money was recovered from the most unusual places.' Such was the force of the blast that some debris was blown over the tops of houses in the next street.

The Red Lion was badly damaged, with furniture, windows and bottles smashed and the pub sign having been blown through the front door. Upstairs there was also damage to the living accommodation and the publican Mr J. Dargue, in his bedroom at the time, received slight injuries. His daughter was in a separate bedroom with her infant child when she heard the bombs coming down. She flung herself on top of her child and protected it from harm although she herself received slight cuts and bruises.

One of the properties next door to the impact zone showed a freak of the effect of blast with a vase of fresh flowers standing completely unharmed although the room had been blown apart. The people quickly rallied and a defiant spirit was evident. An appeal from the head warden for additional volunteers to aid the rescue squads was quickly and enthusiastically answered. A newsagent's which had been open at the time of the attack and suffered damage remained open afterwards and numbers of customers 'waded their way through an assortment of rubble to the counters to purchase as usual their daily newspaper'. Those who had been unfortunate enough to have been bombed out were quickly taken to the local rest centre where they were given food and drink. Shortly after the scene had been cleared, the house in which the bunch of flowers stood soon had a Union Jack fluttering outside and several other properties which were evacuated had large 'V' signs painted on exposed walls by their owners.

The early warning system appears not to have worked in this attack possibly because the aircraft had flown at very low level. A Home Guardsman who was on duty nearby reported that the aircraft had circled the town for some time before heading out to sea and then returning for a dive bombing attack. A warden reported the aircraft skimming the rooftops from the direction of the sea. The warden also said that he 'did not for one minute think it was an enemy plane but thought it was one of our machines in trouble'.[88]

Six days after this attack German bombers revisited Northumberland. Bombs were dropped at Askew Crescent, Tweedmouth, where a 14-year-old girl, Margaret Lough, was killed and two other people injured, at Ryal (no injuries), and further south at Pegswood. The bombing at Tweedmouth resulted in one destroyed house, another badly damaged and thirty slightly damaged. Gas, water and electricity supplies were also disrupted. As the plane fled, two naval patrol boats which were in dock opened fire on it causing the aircraft to circle back and attempt to bomb them too (unsuccessfully).

The bombs which killed Miss Lough landed in gardens beside a row of houses and it was 'a wonder that more people were not injured'.[89] Once again the rescue squads, police and ARP workers were quickly on the scene extricating the injured from the wreckage of their houses. The people affected remained resolute; the next day a postman was delivering letters to several of the bombed houses.

There were several tales of lucky escapes with Mr Logan and his family who lived next door to Miss Lough having perhaps the most miraculous. Mr Logan was awake in the bedroom with his two sons when machine gun fire came through the window and he heard the bombs falling. He quickly threw himself on top of his youngest son to shield him and all six inhabitants were later dug out relatively unhurt despite the fact that the house had been almost demolished. In another example of courage, a Mrs Young threw herself over her blind husband to protect him from the blast as the ceiling of their bedroom collapsed. The two managed to crawl from the wreckage of their home.[90]

At 9.30 pm on 23 August one of these raiders paid the price and was shot down into the sea. The aircraft in question was a Heinkel HE III H-5 (3691) of Kampfgeschwader (Bomber Wing) 26. The bomber was engaged on an anti-shipping mission when it was engaged and shot down by a British destroyer north of Holy Island. The four-man crew took to their dinghy and were rescued, becoming prisoners of war.[91]

As the war continued, shortages became ever more acute. One vital material for fighting the war was timber. Necessary for fortifications, for the construction of aircraft, ships and other items the country was desperately short of skilled men who could cut and haul timber. As a result, men of the Royal Engineers were formed into timber companies and put to work in the forests of Northumberland; even so, this was not enough. Engineers from the colonies and dominions were also formed into timber companies and put to work. The work was dangerous and with the increased urgency accidents were more common than in peacetime. One man to lose his life far from home in north Northumberland was Sapper John Wolstenholme of the 1st Forestry Company, Royal Australian Engineers. A married man from Queensland, Sapper Wolstenholme lost his life on 1 May and was buried at Alnwick Cemetery.

For women the war created opportunities which would have been unthinkable in peacetime, but their role on the battlefield remained contentious throughout the war. Except in a limited few cases, such as manning anti-aircraft batteries or acting as Special Operations Executive agents in occupied Europe, women remained largely confined to a non-combatant role. Despite this the determination of many young women to play what they saw as an active role supporting the combat arms led to massive expansions of the Women's Auxiliary Air Force, Wrens, and Auxiliary Territorial Service. Recruitment into the ATS was brisk in Northumberland with many young women attracted by the wide variety of roles which were offered. Trials in early 1941 had resulted in the revelation that women could serve on searchlight sites and from July entire searchlight regiments became 'mixed' with a large number consisting of a majority of female personnel. Later in the war women were permitted to crew mixed units of anti-aircraft batteries. Another appeal of the ATS was the fact that from July 1941 the women of the service were no longer classed as volunteers but were given full military status. Recruitment campaigns continued throughout the year with women urged to volunteer before service was made compulsory in December 1941 by the Military Service Act. Towns such as Berwick set a target of 500 volunteers for the ATS and recruitment campaigns in the local press showed the variety of roles and duties such as searchlight operator, theodolite operator, driver, mechanic, telephone operator and caterer.

A visit by the ATS's Honorary Controller-Commandant in October helped the recruitment campaign. Mary, Princess Royal and Countess of Harewood, visited an infantry training centre and opened a YWCA hut for the use of members of the ATS. After inspecting the Royal Scots and talking to several of the servicemen the Princess and her entourage moved on to inspect the

ATS recruitment adverts appeared regularly in the local press.

cookhouse and dining hall where she talked with the cooks and praised the meat pies which were being prepared for that day's lunch. The Princess also visited the hospital wing where she conversed with both the staff and patients before completing her tour with an inspection of an ambulance driven by a Miss M. Swan. Moving on to her second engagement of the day the Princess was introduced to several local dignitaries. After opening and inspecting the hut the Princess declared that she was very pleased to open the hut as she was keenly aware of the good service provided by the YWCA to women who were in the services. In the speeches which followed the hut was formally named the Melbourne Hut and it was explained to the Princess that the money for the hut had been sent from Australia and that the town had been chosen as the head of the local ATS camp was

Mary, Princess Royal, an advocate of the ATS (Public Domain).

an Australian. Speaking on behalf of the ATS, Company Sergeant Major Glass praised the hut (which was a large building) and the YWCA before thanking the Princess. Keenly interested in the local ATS the Princess spoke at length to CSM Glass and upon inquiring how long she had served in the ATS was informed that the CSM had joined up at the very start of the war.

For a number of these young women their patriotism resulted in their deaths. In September, Aircraftwoman 1st Class Margaret Henrietta Dixon of Berwick-upon-Tweed died as a member of the WAAF; she served at RAF Elvington in Yorkshire and is buried in her home town.

We saw in the previous chapter just how valuable the work of the WLA was to the agricultural industry in north Northumberland and how one of the biggest problems was finding suitable accommodation for the young volunteers. By April a second hostel at Pawston had been added to the one at Haugh Head in Wooler. While the Haugh Head hostel was solely run by the WLA (indeed it was the first to be so run) the new one was run by the YWCA. At both hostels wardens were employed to care for the young women (no doubt also to monitor their behaviour) and to make their surroundings as pleasant as possible.

Motor transport was hired to transport the women to their places of work on a daily basis.

Attitudes towards the volunteers of the WLA had also softened with most farmers now being appreciative of the efforts of the women. In April *Farmer and Stockbreeder* commented that the WLA was 'an indispensable feature of the war effort. Whatever may be said of women's capacity, no one will deny their zeal and willingness ... They [women] are not capable of all farm work, but the discerning farmer can find use for their services and find these services useful when well directed.'[92]

A meeting of Rothbury Police Court in early October heard a case from September in which it was alleged that a naval officer had assaulted a Forestry Commission worker. On the morning of 9 September two forestry workers, Leonard Spiers and John Wardle, were sent to Harwood to repair the water supply to another Forestry Commission worker's house. When they arrived they went to neighbouring cottages to inform them that the water supply would be turned off for two hours but one of the residents, Charles H. Benfield, objected and came out into the street where Mr Spiers was standing in a trench preparing to begin work. After a short and aggressive conversation Mr Benfield grabbed Mr Spiers by the neck and struck him several times in the face. Mr Wardle then threatened Benfield with a spade and told him to stop but after Spiers climbed out of the trench Benfield attempted to strike him again whereupon Spiers struck out in self-defence and knocked Benfield out. Spiers then asked his co-worker to inform the police and an investigation was carried out after which Benfield was charged with assault. Witnesses confirmed that Benfield was noted for his aggressive character and that on the morning in question he had been in a particularly foul mood. The bench, headed by Lord Armstrong, found Mr Benfield, who was by then on active service as a lieutenant commander, guilty and fined him £2 with an additional £1 in costs.

A few days after the above case had been heard came the death of one of Northumberland's most recognisable members of the aristocracy when Lord Armstrong died after falling while holding a horse at his home at Cragside. Lord Armstrong (the Right-Honourable William Henry Fitzpatrick Watson-Armstrong) was well known throughout the county for his kindness, generosity and charitable works. He had been married three times (the final time to Miss Kathleen England in 1935) and left behind a son, William John Montagu Watson-Armstrong, to carry on the line. Just before 1 pm on Saturday, 11 October, Lord Armstrong and one of his grooms (Joseph Irving Broatch) were holding two riding horses outside The Cottage, Cragside, when the horse being held by Lord Armstrong spooked and shied away causing Lord Armstrong to lose his balance and be dragged a short distance. His doctor attended him and diagnosed a dislocated left shoulder and shock. Despite constant monitoring, Lord Armstrong died on 15 October and was buried at Rothbury on 18 October.

One of the more unusual crimes to be heard in the rural courts at the time was one which could have severely impacted the area's food supply. A local farmer, Mr Edward Cuthbert of Cockshott, Longframlington, admitted that he had bled the carcass of a bullock which he suspected may have died of anthrax. The spread of such a communicable disease at a time when food supplies were stretched to their utmost could have been catastrophic. Mr Cuthbert claimed that he did not know it was wrong to bleed the carcass but in court was told that, in the opinion of the bench, every farmer knew this and, although the bullock was later found to have died from another cause, he was subsequently fined 10s.

Similarly, a Bothal lorry driver was charged with not having cleansed his wagon after dropping off a load of lambs in Rothbury. The police officer who observed the truck drive off without going through the washing and disinfecting machine later saw it return with a second load and he spoke to the driver, cautioning him. When brought before the bench the accused, Mr Arthur Fawkes, replied that the farmers were in a hurry and he did not think he had time to wash the vehicle and then return in time to haul a second load. This was not an adequate excuse as the authorities were, rightly, concerned over the possible spreading of communicable diseases at a time of war and Mr Fawkes was also fined 10s.

A case of careless driving was heard at the same sitting. The incident had taken place at Pauperhaugh when Mr George Elliott Renwick, a farmer from Canada Farm, Longframlington, had driven his car into a telephone kiosk narrowly missing several pedestrians who were waiting on the pavement for a bus. Mr Renwick had been driving from Rothbury in the direction of Weldon Bridge when he took a corner too fast and ran off the road into the kiosk. When the police arrived Mr Renwick 'did not seem to realise what had taken place' and did not reply when Sergeant Cruickshank said he would be charged with dangerous driving (this was later changed to the lesser charge of careless driving). The bench said the matter was an extremely serious one and fined Mr Renwick £4 and endorsed his licence.

We have seen how the efforts of the volunteers who manned the civil defence services were widely appreciated by the people of Northumberland but an appeal made at Amble in November hints at some lack of unity and spirit. The chair of Amble Urban Council (Councillor R. Brown) stated that the civil defence services in the area were undermanned and that there were a number of residents who, though fit and able, had not elected to volunteer in any way. This, he felt, was unacceptable in the current circumstances and he urged these 'slackers' to come forward and 'get into one service or another'.[93]

The appeal was more than likely influenced by the events of the night of 8 November when a German aircraft dropped two bombs on the coastal village of Alnmouth; one bomb struck and destroyed a house in Argyle Street while the other exploded in the road. The bombs resulted in several casualties and hours later rescue squads were still attempting to rescue four adults and three children who were believed trapped. In total three houses were completely demolished, a further eleven were damaged so as to be rendered uninhabitable, others received varying degrees of damage, and the telephone lines were brought down on the south side of the village. As was common after such an event there were attempts to lay the blame. Some suggested that buses parked at the terminus in Argyle Street had left their headlights switched on, while the bus company claimed that personnel in nearby military billets were to blame for showing lights. Once the wreckage had been cleared away, six women and one man were confirmed dead. The fatalities (all at Argyle Street) were: Major (ret) William King Noel Hawks (78) and Isabella Nesbit (47) of Clifton Lodge; Mary Alice Hirst (94) and Mrs Margaret Sofia Little (34) of Beechwood; Mrs Mary Stanton (73) and Ms Irene Collingwood Stanton (39) of Lindisfarne; and Jane Gibb (69) of Glencairn. For a small village like Alnmouth the shock of such losses brought the war into immediate focus.

Losses both civilian and military continued throughout the war with the Army, RAF, Navy and merchant service all losing men from north

Northumberland. Berwick-born Able Seaman Vaughan Robert Weatherly's parents experienced the agony of losing their son in October when his corvette was sunk off Gibraltar by a submarine. Having grown up in the town, Able Seaman Weatherly had worked at a florist's and then with the Shell Mexico Petrol Company before he joined the Royal Navy aged just sixteen in 1937. On 18 October a telegram arrived announcing that Seaman Weatherly was missing in action. His parents then received a letter from their son at their St. Cuthbert's Street home on 21 October. The letter was dated 9 October but, tragically, their son had already been dead for a week when they received this last letter. A further letter arrived on the same day which was from the Commodore at Gibraltar stating that there was no hope of Seaman Weatherly's surviving. Able Seaman Weatherly was aged 21 at the time of his death and only three weeks previously he had been granted the Freedom of the Borough. His ship, HMS *Fleur-de-Lys*, had successfully escorted a convoy to Gibraltar and returned to the Straits to hunt for U-Boats which had shadowed the convoy, but just after 3.30 am on the morning of the 14 October a torpedo fired by *U-206* hit the Flower Class corvette on her port side under the bridge.[94] The explosion detonated the magazine, the ship quickly broke in two and sank in minutes; of the crew of seventy-three there were only three survivors.

Throughout the year the situation caused by food rationing was beginning to reach critical levels and the government and local

HMS Samphire, *sister ship to HMS* Fleur-de-Lys *(Public Domain).*

authorities were looking for alternatives which would allow people (especially those engaged in important work) to have access to nourishing meals. Perhaps the most successful of these enterprises was the establishment of numerous 'British Restaurants' which gave nutritious and cheap meals at low cost to customers. In Alnwick a British Restaurant was opened by the Duchess of Northumberland and was an immediate success in the town. Councillor Stone declared that as a regular customer he could vouch for the service and said that many workmen used the restaurant between 12 and 1 pm and that others who had more flexible lunch hours should stagger their visits. Councillor Stone declared that the manageress was very efficient and that the waitresses 'were nippy and cheerful'.[95]

A side-effect of the rationing system and subsequent shortages of some non-rationed goods was an increase in the phenomenon of queuing. Such was the extent of queues that they rapidly became something of a problem to those in authority; they were anxious that they led to the spread of rumours and encouraged idleness. In early August the local press carried an article which claimed that the problem was a distinctly British one which had been exacerbated by the shortages of non-rationed goods such as canned goods, chocolate and biscuits along with seasonal items such as tomatoes. The article hinted that a possible solution being considered by the Minister of Food was to extend the rationed goods list to include some of these items. The article also urged people to maintain a sense of perspective when it came to rationed goods and claimed that rationed items 'will wait until you call for them'. This ignored the effects that black market activities and shortages sometimes had with numerous examples of stores running out of even rationed items when they clearly should not have.

Throughout the year most local and national newspapers ran regular columns on agriculture and horticulture aimed at professional farmers and the enthusiastic amateur. In May the *Morpeth Herald* ran an article praising the efforts already made by the farming community in restoring great swathes of land to productivity; it claimed that 3,750,000 acres had been ploughed up and that productive crop acres had increased from pre-war levels by between 28 per cent and 40 per cent. The article went on, however, to state that some farmers still seemed to be lagging and were not taking the national situation seriously enough. It claimed that the uptake of the ample supplies of nitrogen and sulphate fertilisers made available by the government remained very poor. Farmers were also encouraged to make use of catch crops instead of allowing their land to lie fallow for long periods between main crops. The article went on to urge farmers to use harvested land for the growing of green fodder crops such as kale, Italian rye grass or green turnips to replace lost grazing land which had been ploughed up. For the amateur enthused by the 'Dig for Victory' campaign, advice was offered not only on the growing of vegetables but also on raising livestock. Hens and rabbits were immensely popular but so were pigs and pig clubs sprang up in every town and village in Northumberland. The same article in the *Morpeth Herald* concluded with some advice to those who had started keeping a pig or two. Research at an agricultural college had revealed that pigs could be successfully reared on a mix of meal with young grass clippings from the lawn (although care had to be taken not to give them too much grass). The writer, under the pen-name Agricola, advised that a normal rate of growth could be maintained by adding such lawn clippings (as a wet slop mixed with meal) to a daily allowance of no more than 2½ lbs per pig.

We have already seen how some members of the community took to poaching in order to obtain food supplies; this continued through 1941. On 1 July a Bishop Auckland man, Arthur V. Knight, who was employed by the Forestry Commission on the banks of the River Alwin, was observed by a local shepherd, Mr William Cook, paddling in the river and splashing in an effort to force fish into an area where he had placed three nets. When Mr Cook asked him what he was doing Knight answered that he was getting trout. Mr Cook then informed him that it was illegal and when Knight became abusive he forcibly took possession of the nets and reported Knight to the bailiffs. The case went before the magistrates, to whom Knight wrote saying that he was innocent, that the nets were not in his possession but merely lying at the bottom of the river and that he was being prosecuted out of vindictiveness. However, the poaching of salmon and trout were becoming a concern to the authorities who now wished to make harsher examples than they had earlier in the war. The solicitor acting for the prosecution thanked Mr Cook and said that such public spiritedness was vital at this time when 'bailiffs are being called up for active service'. The bench concurred in the seriousness of the offence and fined Mr Knight the sum of £2.

In December a Felton haulage contractor, Mr George Norman Birkley, was charged with possession of poaching equipment (a gaff) with the intent to illegally kill salmon, trout or other fish on 1 November. A water bailiff had seen blood at the river bank and when the trail was followed two men were spotted attempting to hide; one of the men was carrying a twelve foot stick with a gaff on the end. The two men made a run for it but the bailiff pursued and apprehended the defendant before cautioning him that possession of a gaff was illegal as was the taking of fish out of season. Mr Birkley pleaded not guilty and said that he had business with the miller (whose garden lay next to the mill race) and that as the miller was not in he had decided to take a walk along the river to pass the time. After encountering the bailiff, he claimed that he told him the reason for his presence and that, because the other man had got away, he was being made a scapegoat. Evidence from Mr Reeney of Woodburn House, West Thirston, would seem to have called into question the timescale of supposed events as he claimed that he saw the bailiff go past with the stick earlier than he had said. Despite this the court found Mr Birkley guilty of possession of the gaff but that he had not been seen using it and fined him the sum of £4 8s 6d.

CHAPTER FOUR

1942
A People's War?

The year got off to a bad start for the residents of Spittal when a lone German raider managed to sneak in undetected at low level to machine gun and bomb the town on 20 January. The streets were busy at the time with people going about their business and many women shopping. The bomber came in just above the rooftops machine gunning the streets below. It then climbed and dropped its bombs before heading back out to sea at speed. Fortunately the machine gunning did little damage causing only minor injuries despite many people coming out of their houses to watch, but the bombs hit a residential street, Sandstell Road, demolishing two houses (Nos. 20 and 22), and damaged many more. Three people were killed. One of the dead, 27-year-old Miss Catherine Robertson, had been out all morning and had only just returned home via the butcher's to do some washing and prepare a meal for her father when he finished work when a bomb hit and demolished her house killing her and her aunt, Miss Margaret Brown (73). Her father would ordinarily have been at home but had agreed to carry on at work for a while longer and this had probably saved his life. He arrived at the scene to find his house demolished and desperate ARP workers, helped by soldiers and airmen, frantically attempting to dig out any survivors from the wreckage. The other fatality was a neighbour, John Roughead (62).

The ARP services carried out sterling work in response to this incident, the female wardens in particular. Police officers, wardens, rescue workers, civilian volunteers and a number of soldiers and airmen who were at home on leave all helped to dig out those who were trapped. When rescue men entered one of the houses which had been severely damaged they found that there were no occupants but then, alerted by a faint cry, they found two dust covered kittens crawling towards them and then a goldfish swimming in its bowl which was now full of dust; all three were rescued.

A Mr William Patterson was out shooting cormorants at the time the enemy aircraft overflew the town and it was so low that he even took a shot at it with his rifle. Mr Patterson returned home to find his house had been damaged. His wife had had a lucky escape when she had been showered with glass and stone.

Amongst the injured was Mr Barty Lough who had experienced two previous raids. Mr Lough was working in the street nearby when he was struck in the back by debris; fortunately he was not seriously injured. Another group of men had been drinking in a nearby pub when the blast blew in a plate glass window and showered them with shards. None were seriously injured although 'more than one glass of beer was lost in the excitement of the moment'.

Mrs G. Ellis was one of those women who were out in the town shopping when the German approached. Mrs Ellis remarked to a friend that it was flying rather low for a British aircraft. At that moment the enemy aircraft opened fire and Mrs Ellis was forced to run for it. Attempting to take shelter in a nearby butcher's shop she was blown into the doorway when the bombs detonated but was relatively unhurt.

The casualties could have been far worse had it not been for the presence of mind of a local headmaster. Hearing the aircraft and knowing that the children were outside the school he immediately went to the door and urged them back inside to take cover under their desks with the result that they were left unscathed by the attack.

The people of the town reacted with determined courage and when asked if they were going to be evacuated one elderly gentleman whose house had been badly damaged replied, 'Not likely … this is our home and not even "Jerry" can take it away from us. We're staying here until the house falls down on top of us.'[96]

Raids like this, so called 'tip and run' attacks carried out by small numbers of aircraft, were a constant threat and meant that guards could not be dropped in the coastal communities of Northumberland. The Luftwaffe was at this time attempting these raids on a regular basis using JU88 bombers; one had attempted to raid Tyneside on the 16 January but was shot down off Tynemouth and on the 19th another had been shot down by Spitfires off Whitby. This one raid destroyed two houses, damaged a further twenty-six and caused considerable damage to the chemical works of Johnstone & Darling as well as the town's gas supply, water mains and telephone wires. Further attempts were made on the night of 31 January/1 February when aircraft attacked Eyemouth and Berwick with bombs and machine guns; three people were slightly injured but the damage was slight. This was followed by another raid four nights later when damage was done at Scremerston; one person, Mr Robert Black, was badly injured. Village store owners Mr and Mrs George Tait were in a neighbouring town at the cinema having left their two children (aged 8 and 5) in the care of a nurse at home but were summoned back. They found their house wrecked and their store damaged. Thankfully, the two children and the nurse were alive after having been rescued from the wreckage. Alan, the 5-year-old, was the most seriously injured, with minor burns. Four nights later another raid was launched with at least one aircraft penetrating further into Northumberland. Several bombs were dropped at Tweedmouth and, although there were no fatalities, a number of properties were damaged and several people injured; the attack also led to disruption as the LNER line was suspended for a time. Several nights later it was the turn of the Amble district to be attacked. A lone aircraft dropped several high explosive bombs on Radcliffe causing four deaths and a further twenty-one casualties. Three of the deaths occurred at New Buildings in Radcliffe with the victims, from an extended family, being Gertrude Rae Craggs (32), Ian MacDonald Craggs (5) and Isabella Appleby MacDonald (59). The final victim of this raid was at 18 Long Row North where Richard William Moffatt (70) was killed.

The police and ARP workers were constantly on alert and were stretched by the series of small raids launched on the north east coast during January and February. One police officer, Constable John Jefferson of Alnmouth, was awarded the British Empire Medal for his bravery in directing rescue operations during a raid in which several houses were damaged and set on fire and for rescuing a boy who was trapped when a house collapsed during a raid. PC Jefferson was a veteran officer having been a member of Northumberland Constabulary for almost thirty years, seeing service at Morpeth, Gosforth, Hexham, Newburn, Wallsend, Berwick and Alnmouth. A native of Newbiggin-by-the-Sea he had, as a young man, worked as a lumberjack and miner in Canada before returning home to join the police force. During the

First World War he had joined the RNVR where he had served in the Mediterranean. No stranger to heroics and a keen swimmer Jefferson had been awarded a certificate from the Royal Humane Society in 1916 for saving three lives in one week of September 1916.

The arduous and dangerous work carried out by the volunteers of the warden service and the various first aid groups was not only vital to the safety of the people of Northumberland but also served as a significant morale boost. Although there was some resentment of the wardens when they at times became rather heavy handed when dealing with relatively minor breaches of the blackout regulations, the majority of people had seen how effective they were in the wake of an air raid and respected them.

Many of those in positions of authority in the ARP organisation did a wonderful job but others let themselves down by letting their position go to their head. The ARP organiser for the Northern Area of Northumberland, Mr David William Errington Brock, fell victim to this when he was prosecuted for breaching the Defence Regulations Act by commenting on the movement of British troops in an incident on 26 December 1941. While out hunting on Boxing Day Mr Brock, of Rayheugh, Chathill, had commented on a raid on the Norwegian coast. Mr Brock had been aware of the raid in advance but claimed he thought it had already taken place when he spoke. Mr Brock was accused of having told Colonel Milvain and Miss Ruth Wilkinson that a raid was to take place during which British troops would hand out Christmas presents to Norwegian children while part of a group hunting at Newlands; he claimed the raid would take place that day (26th December).

After the matter came to the attention of the police, the Chief Constable, Mr Studdy, interviewed Mr Brock on 31 December and the accused admitted that he had prior knowledge of the raid but said that he thought it would take place on the day that he mentioned it. The next day the Chief Constable and a military officer interviewed the accused once more and asked the name of his informant. Mr Brock replied that he was not prepared to give the name of his informant as 'he realised that he was guilty of an indiscretion and he would not allow his foolishness to get a friend into trouble'. Mr Brock was cautioned as to the nature of his offences and told that refusing to give the name of his informant would result in a further charge; he was then given time to rethink and, if necessary, communicate with his informant.

Two days later Mr Brock was again interviewed and he confessed that on 22 December he had been sitting in a car outside a shop in Berwick when he overheard two soldiers discussing the forthcoming raid. On Christmas Day he spoke to a naval officer of his acquaintance and asked him about the raid. The officer denied any knowledge of such an operation but Mr Brock made it explicit that he did not believe him and the officer then confirmed that the raid was to take place but said to Mr Brock, 'For goodness sake keep your mouth shut because it does not come off until 8.30 tomorrow morning.'[97] Despite this warning Mr Brock had taken the opportunity to discuss the raid while out hunting thinking that it had already taken place.

Although the prosecution admitted that there was no question of Mr Brock's loyalty, he had been incredibly indiscreet and had jeopardised the security of the operation and the lives of the soldiers, sailors and airmen taking part in the raid. The indiscretion was compounded by the fact that Mr Brock was a former commissioned army officer and indeed was still one as in addition to his ARP duties he was commanding officer of a local Home Guard unit.

After hearing the evidence the bench retired and came back with a guilty verdict. They declared that it was 'unfortunate' that their views as to the seriousness of such offences did not always coincide with those of the Home Secretary who had, in the past, reduced fines handed down by them for similar offences. They viewed the matter extremely seriously and imposed a fine of £20 plus £5 5s in costs.

The operation in question was Operation Archery, the raid on Vaagso. The raid was a combined operation involving, for the first time, all the services, with RAF Hampden bombers laying smoke screens and harassing enemy airfields while Beaufighters and Blenheims maintained patrols to restrict the activities of enemy aircraft. Met by a Royal Navy submarine, several warships and two landing craft mounted the attack which was undertaken by soldiers from 2, 3, 4 and 6 Commandos along with a detachment from the Royal Norwegian Army. The raid succeeded in destroying coastal defences, radio transmitters, stores, a power station, a lighthouse, oil and fish oil factories and 15,000 tons of merchant shipping. The German forces lost four Heinkel bombers, 150 troops killed and 98 captured. Additionally, 71 Norwegians volunteered to take passage back to the

Commandos in action at Vaagso (Public Domain).

UK where they could aid in the war effort. Perhaps the greatest success was that it persuaded Hitler to strengthen defences in Norway at the expense of France; some 30,000 German troops were moved to Norway, most from manning the Atlantic Wall. Against this was the loss of 51 soldiers, sailors and airmen killed, and 7 Blenheims, 2 Beaufighters and 2 Hampdens lost.

Class matters were one again brought to the fore in mid-January when Glendale Rural Council met at Wooler to discuss the recent appointment of Lady Tankerville, of Chillingham Castle, to the bench as a Justice of the Peace. The majority of councillors, led by Councillor J. Phillips, were vehemently against the appointment, which had been made by the Lord Lieutenant, of yet another member of the gentry to this position. Councillor Phillips argued that the bench had 'been the preserve of the landed classes for years' and decried the fact that a tradesman or worker had no chance of being appointed. Any whose political views were not 'Tory' would also be automatically excluded (as several had been). Councillor Phillips saw the closed shop mentality as being 'a slur and insult to the eligible women in Wooler and Glendale who could fill the post with distinction'. His pronouncements attracted agreement from a majority of the councillors present, notably T.B. Ford and G. Gallon. Phillips continued by stating that the appointment had met with a barrage of complaints locally and that it had further eroded confidence in the bench. It seems that over recent years a great deal of faith had been lost in the members of the bench and in their judgements and this appointment was the final straw. The matter also had a nationalistic flavour, not surprising given the state of wartime Britain, because, as Councillor Phillips pointed out, Lady Tankerville was a Swede by birth and had spent a great deal of her childhood in Sweden. Indeed he made a point of highlighting his belief that Lady Tankerville was 'a Swede by birth, by education, by upbringing and probably by tendencies'. He argued that even though she might have many fine qualities it was solely the fact of the class she had married into which had seen her appointed, saying that 'had she married the keeper of the wild cattle at Chillingham instead of the owner she would never have been put on the bench'; a statement which once again drew praise from Councillor Ford. The Clerk, Mr R. Middlemas, seems to have been more reluctant to interfere as he stated that the appointment of JPs to the bench had 'absolutely nothing whatever to do' with the council and he baldly told the councillors, 'You, as a Council, have absolutely nothing to do with it.' Phillips and his supporters were not to be so easily put off and stated that although they realised they had nothing to do with the appointment as a body, they still had the right to lodge a complaint with the Lord Lieutenant. Councillor Phillips stated that the council 'ought to have' the right to appoint or nominate and advise on candidates. In the short debate which followed, one of the female councillors, Mrs Tweddell, mentioned that she knew that 'several names have been sent up from the Glendale district and they have been turned down'.[98] When the vote was taken it was decided to put their complaints before the Lord Lieutenant by ten votes to two. However it does not appear to have made any difference – I can't find any further mention of the story and Lady Tankerville continued in the role!

The issue of class once again reared its head over the issue of the donation of metal to the war effort. While the majority of organisations and individuals had gladly donated metal railings and other goods with the (often mistaken) belief that they would be used directly in the war effort, it seems that there was some resentment at what was seen as hanging back by some members of the landed classes in the county. Glendale District Council heard that there was dispute over railings which were possibly of historic value. It seems that the council surveyor had undertaken a survey and decided that no railings in the area fell within the definition of historically valuable as defined by central government. However, an official from the Ministry of Works and Buildings had said that she thought the gates at Lilburn Tower and Ford Castle should be preserved. There followed a letter from a Mr Sale on behalf of Lord Joicey regarding the gates and railings at Ford Castle and Etal Manor. In his letter Mr Sale stated that while Lord Joicey objected to the removal of the gates at both properties, he had agreed to the removal of some railings but that he expected payment for these. A similar letter had been received from Mr E.F. Collingwood of Lilburn Tower. The Salvage Officer, Councillor J.G. Beattie, objected to the tone of both letters and reiterated his opinion, in public, that none of the railings were of historical value as defined by the Act as they had been manufactured after 1820. He also asked who Mr Sale was and under what authority he had given approval for the removal of some railings but not others and concluded by asking the clerk to write to Mr Sale telling him that his appeal was too late.

The removal of railings could indeed prove contentious especially when the contractors employed acted speedily, sometimes without due care, or adopted a high-handed attitude with local officials or landowners. In May Berwick's MP, Captain G.C. Grey, became involved when he was forced to concede that damage had been done to a property in Berwick when railings were removed. Captain Grey wrote to the Parliamentary Secretary for the Ministry of Works to ask him to ensure that in future when railings were to be removed from Berwick that the contractors should first get in touch with the county surveyor to determine how best to proceed. Captain Grey was, however, at pains to point out that sentimentality had no place in such decisions as 'The war is so serious ... that we must be prepared to give up the metal, no matter where it is situated, if the Ministry of Supply needs it.'[99] Captain Grey added that workmen should be encouraged to do a good job; if they did not then the repairs would have to be paid for and would be charged to the guilty contractor.

We have already seen how easy it was to become criminalised due to the host of new laws and regulations that had been brought in during the war. Many of these new orders were designed to control items of food so as to prevent them from going into black market channels. Rothbury rabbit dealer Andrew Tully fell afoul of one of these regulations in April and May when he was accused of illegally selling 432 rabbits between Rothbury and North Shields on three occasions. Mr Tully had not applied for a collector and wholesaler's licence (he claimed he was not even aware of the need for such a licence) and that he had not kept a record of those he had sold the rabbits to. Although the bench did have some sympathy they pointed out that as Mr Tully had been in business for over twenty years he should have known about the licencing rules; they fined Mr Tully the sum of £6 4s.

A few months later another Northumberland man found himself being fined for contravening the Rabbits (Control and Maximum Prices) Order. Mr Andrew Little of New Moor House, Longframlington, was described as a small farmer who caught some rabbits and sold them at Morpeth. Mr Little was charged with two offences: selling 110 lbs of rabbits for £4 2s 6d on 20 February, and selling 200 lbs of rabbits for £4 17s 6d on 11 March. His solicitor claimed that although Mr Little pleaded guilty he had contacted the Ministry to see if a licence was required and was ignorant of the scale of regulation. Mr Little was fined 10s with £2 2s in costs.

The women of the Land Army were now proving their value to agriculture in Northumberland with many farmers now willing to take advantage of this additional form of labour. The women undertook almost every role on the farm including the strenuous activities such as harvesting, shearing and dipping sheep. Without their contribution it is certain that output in Northumberland would have decreased as more men left for the services.

In the spring of 1942 it became clear that the number of men who had joined up and had formerly been employed in felling timber was resulting in a slump in the availability of this precious wartime resource. Thus the government announced the formation of the Women's Timber Corps (WTC) whose volunteers quickly became

*Women from the Land Army dipping sheep at East Shaftoe (*Daily Mirror).

known as Timber Jills. The WTC would work in forestry and in sawmills and were told in advance that the work would be arduous and dirty. Despite this, volunteers came forward in numbers and the WTC was placed under the command of the WLA (of which it was officially a part). Members faced a six-week training period before being posted to a billet and undertaking their duties (which included felling, loading, driving tractors, working with horses and operating sawmills among other things); for undertaking this extremely heavy work the women were paid between 35 and 46 shillings per week (although deductions for food, etc, reduced this significantly).

Petrol rationing had a knock-on effect on health care in many of the more remote north Northumberland communities and a letter from Dr James Richard Hewat-Jaboor outlined how in January one of his elderly patients had taken ill and needed hospital treatment but that he had experienced a two-hour delay in securing transportation to Edinburgh Infirmary because he could not find a driver with sufficient petrol coupons. At Dr Jaboor's suggestion the council agreed to maintain an ambulance car throughout the daylight hours to be driven by Mr Atkinson (of the local garage) or one of his workers and a similar car at night organised by a Mr Greathead (presumably a member of the council); both of the ambulance cars would be constantly kept fully supplied with petrol.

The patriotic fervour which characterised much of the wartime home front could sometimes have unfortunate consequences when it led otherwise law abiding civilians to fall afoul of wartime regulations. At Berwick, the harbourmaster David L. Lowden was charged with having arranged a collection in Berwick and several surrounding communities (including Boulmer, Longhoughton, Littlehoughton and Howick) for the purpose of purchasing gifts for the Royal Northumberland Fusiliers Prisoners of War Christmas Parcels Fund. However, it was illegal to mount such a collection, even for charitable purposes, without a licence from the police. Mr Lowden had arranged for a Ms Murray to organise the collection at Longhoughton and had told her that he had police permission but she grew suspicious when he asked her to open the collecting boxes and to send the money on by postal order; Miss Murray refused to do this and instead contacted the police. When questioned, Mr Lowden admitted he had not sought permission and put this down to forgetfulness due to overwork. The police accepted this, informing the bench that they were satisfied that 'there was no question of any allegation of fraud in this case'.[100] Mr Lowden also admitted that the parcels had been sent by him before any money had been collected but was told that only the Red Cross was permitted to send parcels to prisoners of war. Despite the good intentions of the accused, the bench viewed the matter extremely seriously as it breached a law which had been put in place to protect the public from fraud and it was clear that Mr Lowden knew that he was breaking the law. However they did recognise that there was no attempt at committing fraud in this case and thus, despite the maximum possible penalty being six months' imprisonment or a £100 fine, only fined the accused the sum of £5.

Despite such setbacks, charitable and fundraising attempts continued to be incredibly well supported in Northumberland with even the smallest communities making substantial contributions. At Grindon, just south of Norham, the Grindon Work Party could boast that it had, by mid-January, sent some 404 woollen garments to several forces charity depots in the past year (this brought the total number knitted and dispatched to 692). The largest beneficiary was the RAF which received 121 knitted comforts while others included the Northumberland & Durham War Relief Fund (117), Royal Navy (83), King's Own Scottish Borderers (32), Minesweepers (18), Russian Army (14) and nineteen to miscellaneous good causes. The annual meeting also heard how funding was becoming increasingly scarce and hard to obtain but that many friends and members had helped. The fundraising work of the Duddo Youth Service Corps had been particularly encouraging.

Many of the groups which came into being during the war also lent their strength to fundraising activities, with the Home Guard, ARP Services and nursing services all playing their part. In early January the Berwick Home Guard, for example, held a dance with a prize ceremony and refreshments. The venue was the Drill Hall and the majority of the funds raised were donated to the Queen's Nurses.

ARP arrangements in the Alnwick district came under scrutiny in June when the County Council recommended that the local office of the ARP controller for Alnwick district be abolished and the work undertaken by the administrative staff of Alnwick Rural District Council. Along with this it was suggested that the organisation's headquarters be moved from the coastal village of Warkworth to the more centrally located council offices at Alnwick. While this seems to have been an eminently sensible suggestion and was common practice in most other areas it provoked a rather extreme reaction. The controller (Major T.G. Boss), the chief warden (Councillor T.A. Swallow), and the senior warden at Alnmouth (Brigadier General Strange) offered their immediate resignations. Alnwick RDC disagreed with the suggestions and stated that council staff were already operating under an extremely heavy workload which meant that they would be unable to take on the extra ARP work.

While the Luftwaffe was still mounting sporadic raids over Northumberland, RAF Bomber Command was increasingly striking back at German cities. These night raids were dangerous for the men of the RAF with the German defences increasing in strength and sophistication. A further danger came from the often poor weather conditions encountered upon return to Britain. Navigation aids were basic, the aircraft often returned off-course, and experienced communication difficulties with the ground.

Shortly before midnight on 15/16 January a Vickers Wellington IC (Z1078) of 150 Squadron was attempting to return to its home airfield at Snaith from a mission to Hamburg when it ran into difficulties. The aircraft's radio equipment was unserviceable and it was having difficulties navigating. They wandered north over the Cheviots in snow and heavy mist and, not realising they were over high ground, crashed into West Hill on Cheviot. Local shepherds realised an aircraft had crashed when they smelled burning and John Dagg and two friends set off up the hill with Mr Dagg's sheepdog Sheila.[101] When they reached the crash site one of the six-man crew was dead and the others were injured. The three shepherds

Mr John Dagg and his dog Sheila. The pair rescued survivors after an RAF bomber crashed on Cheviot (courtesy of John Dagg Jnr).

extricated the survivors and managed to alert the authorities. Of the initial survivors, two later succumbed to their injuries.[102]

Losses amongst Bomber Command men from Northumberland were a continuing feature of local newspapers.[103] In April, while news was breaking of the loss of an entire battalion of Royal Northumberland Fusiliers at Singapore, a list of Wooler men was published which chronicled the fate of eleven men from the small community who had either been posted missing or killed; one was from Bomber Command. On the night of 30 March, Air Marshal Harris ordered an attack by thirty-four Halifax bombers on the German battleship *Tirpitz* which was in a fjord near Trondheim. The battleship was very heavily defended and so distant that the aircraft had to take off from RAF Lossiemouth. Weather conditions were far from ideal, leading to the bombers failing to score any hits on the ship. Six Halifaxes were lost with one 10 Squadron aircraft, containing the very experienced crew of Squadron Leader F.D. Webster, DFC, being one. The Halifax II, ZA-F (W1043), was shot down in the target area and its seven-man crew were all killed. Among them was 27-year-old mid-upper air gunner Sergeant Walter Hall who was flying on his 25th operational sortie.[104] The news of their second son's failure to return from the operation was delivered to Mr and Mrs Walter Hall who must have been extremely anxious as they had two other sons who were still on service, one as an NCO with the Royal Marines in the Middle East and the other as a radio operator with the Merchant Navy.

Back on the home front the people of Berwickshire and the Borders were perturbed to hear that an Italian prisoner of war who had been held at Duns had escaped and was assumed to be loose in the nearby countryside. The escapee was quickly recaptured at West Ord after a Lieutenant Moody of the Home Guard in the village of Norham recognised his PoW uniform. More worryingly it transpired that the PoW had safely passed through both Berwick and Tweedmouth without his conspicuous uniform attracting notice.

The change to British Double Summer Time (which meant that Summer Time was two hours in advance of GMT instead of one), combined with the northern latitude of Northumberland, had a peculiar and potentially confusing effect on the blackout times. In England and Wales this resulted in the blackout ending 45 minutes before sunrise and beginning 45 minutes after sunset. However, this did not apply to

Scotland or to Northumberland, Durham and Cumberland because the lighting conditions were so different in these areas.

Despite the many concerns on the Home Front the people of Northumberland were still anxiously following the war and the exploits of their loved ones who were abroad in the forces. In February dire news began to arrive concerning the fate of the 9th Battalion, Northumberland Fusiliers, which had recently departed for the Far East. The disaster which had befallen the regiment's territorials in France in 1940 was repeated with even more dire consequences at Singapore when the entire 9th Battalion was taken prisoner by the Japanese within days of arriving. By early January the battalion was at Bombay and after a gruelling fortnight of training in high temperatures at Deolali the battalion departed for Singapore aboard the French troop ship *Felix Roussel*. While aboard ship the men were given a number of lectures on jungle warfare tactics and on the Japanese as an enemy, while en route they saw a number of Japanese aircraft. On 5 February they were attacked and two fusiliers from 'Y' Company were killed but the *Felix Roussel* docked at Singapore at 11 pm.[105] The battalion went into action the very next day and fought continuously for the next nine days but by 13 February the situation was desperate and ammunition running short. On 15 February the battalion was surrounded by Japanese units. Extremely low on ammunition, at 4 pm they were, amidst great despair, ordered to ceasefire and line up along the Bukit Timah Road to surrender. Robbed of their few possessions by Japanese soldiers, abused and mistreated, they were marched to Changi where they remained in the open for several months before they were moved to Keppel Harbour at Singapore and used as dock labour. A series of moves followed which left the remnants of the battalion at work on the infamous Burma Railroad and the Bridge over the River Kwai. Amongst the many men from the Rothbury area who were taken prisoner was Fusilier Henry J. Scott. Originally from Norham, Henry had worked before the war as a groom at Moorside, Rothbury. In September his parents received a letter from him telling them that he was a prisoner but was well; a great many others were not so fortunate and many members of the battalion died while in captivity while a great many others suffered from illnesses and were left mentally or physically scarred by their experiences.[106]

Many small communities felt the loss of so many men from the 9th

Battalion when it was destroyed at Singapore. Local newspapers carried lists of names which were sadly reminiscent of those from the First World War when 'Pals Battalions' had gone into action on the Somme. For example in April the *Berwick Advertiser* carried a list of ten men who had been posted missing in the fall of Singapore. The list included: Lance Corporal R. Steel of Ryecroft Crescent; Fusilier A. Jackson of Weetwood Avenue; Fusilier D. Tweddle of Ramsay's Lane; A. McIntosh, the only son of Mr and Mrs W.S. McIntosh of Market Place; James Abercrombie of Milfield; W. Brown of Common Road; A.E. Fairnington of West Lodge; and J. Davidson of Weetwood Avenue. The Fairnington family had a particularly fine record of service: seven sons on active service, six in the Army and one in the RAF, while Mr Fairnington senior was a member of the local Home Guard.[107]

All of the men in this list appear to have survived but two Wooler brothers, George and Charles Scott of Ramsay Road tragically did not. Lance Corporal George Scott, 9th Royal Northumberland Fusiliers, was 24 and working on the Burma–Siam railroad when he died on 27 September 1943 just over eighteen months after being taken prisoner at Singapore. His older brother, Private Charles Scott, 9th Royal Northumberland Fusiliers, had died before him, in similar circumstances, on 10 May 1943 aged 29.[108]

At Norham, John and Mary Weatherburn received the news that three of their sons had been posted missing with the 9th Battalion. The three were Corporal John Weatherburn of 'Z' Company and Fusiliers M. and H. Weatherburn. 33-year-old Corporal John Weatherburn did not survive the battle for Singapore and was later confirmed as having been killed in action on 15 February, the day the battalion was forced to surrender.

Prisoners taken earlier in the war were still remembered in Northumberland with civilians, including friends and relatives, keen to raise funds to keep these unfortunates supplied with some essentials despite the privations of German prisoner of war camps. Letters from the men did make it home at times and were eagerly passed amongst Northumbrian communities. In May, Mrs Dunn of Lambton Avenue, Lowick, received a letter from a prisoner, Corporal James L. Robinson, who was in the same hut as her son, Fusilier James Dunn, Royal Northumberland Fusiliers. The corporal described how he was writing on behalf of her son (who would appear from the tone of the letter to have been very young and possibly injured) and the other four men who occupied the same hut. All of the occupants had been taken prisoner at St-Valery in 1940 and consisted of four Northumbrians, a Tynesider and a Lancashire man (Corporal Robinson). The men seem to have been in good spirits and Corporal Robinson paints a cheery cameo of their lives and personalities. He is keen to inform Mrs Dunn that her son is 'well and now is quite able to take care of himself' and of how his companions had taken James 'in hand, and I think I can boast that he is quite a different boy to the one you knew (He can darn his own socks now and also wash his underclothes, so please remember this!)'; he then goes on to 'introduce the boys'. The group's 'clown' and a very cheerful man, John Twaddle of Amble; Dixon Tate of Radcliffe who was known as 'change partners' because of his proclivity for changing girlfriends; John Osmonde of Berwick who was described as 'the fisherman soldier, who pines for the sea'; and George Tague of Gateshead, described as a romantic.[109]

Charitable collections continued apace with Berwick, along with other communities in north Northumberland, holding a 'Wings for Victory' week in April. To open the campaign a speech was given on the steps of the town hall by one of Britain's most successful night fighter pilots, Squadron Leader John Groves Topham DFC. At the time Topham was based at RAF Winfield with 219 Squadron and had been credited with the destruction of two German aircraft and one probable.[110] The officer commented afterwards that he had been extremely nervous in giving his speech and that he could boast of two things in his life: having shot down a German aircraft and having given a speech on the steps of Berwick Town Hall!

The vital importance of the farming industry of rural Northumberland was highlighted by repeated praise of the farmers who in many cases had ploughed up previous pasture and meadowland in order to grow a greater tonnage of arable and vegetable crops. In September the people of the area were told that the potato and root vegetable crop in the county had been extremely good and promised to 'excel all records'. It was not only farmers who came in for praise, so did the many amateur gardeners who had turned over their allotments, gardens and waste ground to producing food during the crisis.

Although we have seen how farmers were encouraged, and in some cases ordered, to plough up pasture land, much of the north Northumbrian terrain did not lend itself to extensive arable production, and the breeding of livestock, particularly sheep and cattle, continued to be extensive. In October, Wooler Livestock Auction Mart Company held its annual sale of cross-Angus and shorthorn suckled calves. Demonstrating the extent and popularity of livestock farming in the area, the sale attracted a catalogue of 650 head. The show was said to be of a high standard with 'many pens of exceptional breeding and condition'. As a result prices and business was very brisk indeed with the sellers being well pleased with the results.

Cross Angus Suckled Calves		
Seller	**£**	**s**
Milfield Hill	12	5
Fenton House	16	10
Way-to-Wooler	13	15
Beanley	13	10
Ancroft North Moor	14	
Wrangham	20	
Grindon	12	5
Chatton (Winter)	12	
Biddlestone Home Farm	13	5
Low Humbleton	12	5
Barmoor Ridge	18	5
Murton White House	17	5
Pawston	16	10
Low Hedgeley	17	15
Healey Farm	18	10
Ingram	20	
Mindrum	13	15
Dancing Hall	16	5
Scremerston Town Farm	14	15
Tritlington	17	5
Milfield Hill	11	5
Low Hedgeley	20	
Tynely	11	15

In the same month, Messrs Robert Donkin Ltd held their annual sale of young bulls, milk cows, heifers and suckled cows at Rothbury. Once again there was a very good attendance and business was brisk although, probably as a result of the sale at Wooler, there were few suckled calves in evidence. Once again prices were satisfactory with a young bull from Fairnley fetching £30 while others were sold for £28 (Carterside) and £24 (Tosson Tower). Milk cows also attracted high prices with the highest being £68 for an in-calf cow from Hepple Whitefield while other calved milk cows were sold for between £34 (Healeycote) and £59 (Lorbottle Steads). Calved and in-calf heifers also saw a brisk trade with prices fluctuating between £29 and £45 10s. In a demonstration of the enthusiasm of the amateur for raising livestock during the war, the Coquetdale Calf Club also sold five dairy heifer calves for prices between £10 and £21.

Calved Heifers for Sale at Rothbury		
Seller	**£**	**s**
Bywell	36	
West Horton (in-calf)	44	
Callaly Mill	29	
Fairnley	36; 40	
Whittingham Grange	32; 37	
Carterside	45	10
West Newtown	36	
West Hills	45	
Tosson Tower	36	

Given the vital importance of food production due to the massive loss of merchant shipping in the Battle of the Atlantic the work of the Northumberland War Agricultural Committee broadened as the war went on. One of the key roles played by the War Ag was in education. Classes were regularly held in which farmers were given advice by regional and national experts. The committee also encouraged some of the regular activities of the farming community. On Boxing Day the committee held its annual ploughing competition at Nafferton but also promoted the demonstrations on tractor maintenance and plough setting which were held throughout the day. The importance of maintaining tractors was becoming ever more essential as farms became increasingly mechanised. In order to ensure a good attendance the committee informed farmers that, because of the importance of food production, and given the educational nature of the event, farmers would be allowed to use their private cars where no alternative was available.

Morpeth Court heard an interesting case in November regarding a crash between a bus used for transporting workmen and an army tank. The accident happened on 17 October at Weldon Bridge near Longframlington and the tank crew insisted that they had halted when the impact occurred. The police agreed that the crew of the tank, which was going northwards, had seen the bus coming down the bank, had halted and that one of them stood up on the turret and waved for the bus to stop. The tank driver, Kenneth Clark, testified that he had seen the bus from approximately eighty yards away, that the driver had a clear view of the tank on the bridge and that it was clear there was insufficient room for the two vehicles as the tank took up eleven and a half feet of the eighteen-foot bridge. Conditions were clear although the road surface was described as wet but not greasy by the police officer who arrived on the scene and he testified that there were no skid marks on the road surface. The defendant, Joseph Norman Raisbeck (45) of Bedlington, claimed that when he had gone onto the bridge his bus had skidded and collided with the tank and the bridge parapet. After some deliberation the bench reduced the charge to careless driving, found the defendant guilty and fined him £2 11s 9d.

In December Doctor Purves reported that there had been a measles epidemic in the Alnwick district. The outbreak had begun in Warkworth but had spread quickly although, thankfully, the strain appeared to be mild and there had been no deaths as a result of the disease. By early December there had been fifty-eight cases reported but Dr Purves stated that although measles could be deadly, indeed Dr Purves had once lost 'nine cases in two days',[111] it seemed to have lost virulence and he did not recommend closing the local schools.

Once again military losses continued in the sometimes heavy fighting and, given the military tradition of many families in the area, it is unsurprising that many received tragic news. A well-known family of the Northumbrian gentry, the Fenwicke-Clennells, with their main seat at Harbottle in Upper Coquetdale, had a long history of military service and had already suffered loss and worry.[112] The family suffered a further loss in the days before Christmas when 19-year-old Pilot Officer Edward Fenwicke-Clennell failed to return from a bombing raid on Munich on 21 December. Serving as a pilot with 9 Squadron, RAF Bomber Command, Edward and his crew had taken off from RAF Waddington in Lancaster I (coded WS-G, W4185) shortly after 5.30 pm as part of a bomber force of 137 aircraft. Nothing further was heard from the aircraft but it became clear that WS-G was one of the eight Lancasters which failed to return that night. It became known after the war that P/O Fenwicke-Clennell's aircraft had been hit by anti-aircraft fire and crashed at Oberschleissheim some sixteen kilometres north of the target.[113] P/O Fenwicke-Clennell and the five members of his crew who lost their lives were buried side-by-side at Oberschleissheim churchyard.[114]

CHAPTER FIVE

1943

Measures of Hope

As the year opened, Rothbury Police Court met with only three minor criminal offences to be heard. Two of these involved lighting offences involving fires which had not been properly extinguished before dark. One was a chaff fire at the property of Richard Jeffreys of Wreighill Farm and the other was a brushwood fire on land owned by John Robert Howe of Bishop Auckland; both were fined £1. The remaining case involved a Middlesex quarryman who was employed at Wardshill Quarry and who was found to be in possession of a brand new pair of army boots for which he had paid £1. The unfortunate quarryman claimed that he needed new boots for work, but he was fined the sum of £2.

The theft or receipt of army property was treated very seriously by magistrates in Northumberland who recognised that such attempts at defrauding the forces were a drain on Britain's wartime economy and were therefore not only criminal but unpatriotic. In January Alnwick magistrates heard how a local married woman, Mrs Ina Porter of 53 Clayport Street, had bought two army blankets worth £1 7s 4d from her soldier brother-in-law for 10s as he had said he was short of money. The blankets had been discovered by Sergeant Frederick Burn of the Military Police and Sergeant Watson of Alnwick Police. Mrs Porter had admitted immediately that they were army blankets but stated that she had believed they were her brother-in-law's property at the time and had thought only to do him a favour as he didn't want them. Mrs Porter added that this would be 'the first time and the last' and added that her brother-in-law had told her that he was hard up at the time. Nevertheless the magistrates fined Mrs Porter the sum of £3 after finding her guilty of receiving the blankets.[115]

Much of the crime resulting from the theft of army clothing occurred because many people were struggling with this aspect of rationing, especially those involved in heavy manual labour. Another crime brought before Alnwick magistrates in January, however, seems to have arisen from the desire of a young man to appear to be a member of the armed forces. The crime had taken place on 21 November 1942 when Sergeant Grey had observed a young man named Quinn on his bicycle wearing an army battledress and a red beret. Knowing that the young man was not in the army the sergeant stopped him and questioned him as to where he had obtained the battledress. He was told that it had been a gift from his father. Sergeant Grey later interviewed the man, timber loader Michael Quinn of 67a St. Thomas' Close, Alnwick, and was told that he had found the blouse in the Market Place and had received the battledress trousers from another of his sons who was currently in the Middle East on active service; Mr Quinn was fined £2 for 'detaining' the battledress.

Poaching for game remained a constant problem throughout the year and at the turn of the year a case was heard at Alnwick of two men, of Netherton Colliery and Bedlington, who had been apprehended with ferrets, nets and several dead rabbits at Lesbury. Once again, the magistrates took a dim view of the affair and the two, Joseph Cavanagh and Walter Ellis, were fined £1 and £2.

As shortages increased more and more people were prosecuted for relatively minor offensives that in peacetime they would not have been. An Ashington bus driver, Harold Smith, fell afoul of the law regulating the use of petrol coupons in January when he faced charges of using his company-owned bus to travel to Shilbottle to see his wife. Mr Smith was employed by an Alnwick-based firm who contracted him to drive a 26-seater bus transporting workmen. Part of his duties involved taking the bus to Ashington to be serviced at the weekends but on this occasion he had been observed deviating from his usual route which took him through the village of Lesbury and instead going via Shilbottle. The constable who observed Mr Smith was suspicious and followed the bus until he found it parked outside a house in Colliers Close, Shilbottle. Upon making inquiries the officer found Mr Smith inside a nearby house with his wife who had been staying there for a few days' holiday. Mr Smith pleaded not guilty and explained to the authorities that he had made the detour after being told that it was no longer than his usual route and would therefore not use any more petrol, and he thought he would pick up his wife to take her back home to Ashington. The magistrates were sympathetic of this technical breach of the rules and agreed that the charge would be dismissed upon the payment of £1 in costs.

A far more serious case involving the alleged black-market trafficking of petrol came before the court at Rothbury in September; 14 men were charged with a total of 26 separate charges. The men were described as a 'Gang of black-marketeers' who had 'entered into a nefarious conspiracy'. The first defendant was one of the suppliers, Matthew Sanderson of Morpeth, a driver for the Morpeth-based haulage contractor Richard Elliott, but many of the conspirators were from the upper Coquetdale area.[116] Mr Sanderson was employed to make regular runs in his lorry between Morpeth and Ewesley Quarry and the local police, who had been aware for some time of the circulation of suspicious petrol supplies, became suspicious of his activities and began investigations. They pinpointed Ewesley Quarry as a possible source and raided the property. During the course of their investigations they discovered that Mr Sanderson and a blacksmith at the quarry, Mr John Campbell of Ritton White House, had entered into a conspiracy in June 1942 whereby they agreed to begin siphoning off petrol from Sanderson's lorry to sell locally. The venture would have been extremely profitable given that Sanderson was making daily journeys to the quarry and the fuel was supplied by the Petroleum Board to his employer.

When Mr Elliott was called to give evidence he testified that Mr Sanderson, who had been employed by him for several years, had visited him shortly after the raid, had confessed that he had been charged with stealing petrol and that he had been siphoning the petrol with a rubber tube at the quarry. Sanderson also confessed to the police and stated that he had been selling the petrol to Mr Campbell for two shillings per gallon. Throughout the period that the scam was running petrol supplies were extremely short and the government had taken a much firmer control of haulage companies which were making regular but necessary journeys.

It would seem that Campbell was the ringleader of the conspiracy as he had initially enticed Mr Sanderson to siphon fuel and had later encouraged another Morpeth driver, Mr Allen Graham Creighton, to do the same. For the two shillings per gallon that Campbell was paying he admitted that he gathered four or five gallons per time. He ludicrously claimed that he had not profited by selling the petrol but that some of the people he had sold it to had 'stood him a few beers'. Campbell claimed that he stole the petrol for altruistic reasons, only to 'oblige a few friends' whom he knew were short on supplies. Such was the seriousness of the allegations that Mr Campbell was told he would face the assizes and was allowed bail set at £25.

The next of the gang to be seen was Mr William Alexander Thompson of Nunnykirk Home Farm, Netherwitton, who was employed as a quarryman at a nearby quarry. He had been approached by Campbell and had agreed to buy petrol from him. Thompson admitted that he had been a regular customer and usually purchased eight gallons per week and, contrary to Campbell's testimony, paid Campbell the sum of 2/6 per gallon. Police testimony, however, revealed the murkier side of the conspiracy when they told the bench that Mr Thompson had confessed that he had initially approached Mr Campbell in May 1942 and told him he was short of petrol before beginning his purchases. Thompson also confessed that he had resold a great deal of the petrol but, once again, claimed that he had made no profit from it and stated that he didn't know why he had done it; Thompson refused to speak in court.

Next was the turn of the other driver in the conspiracy, Creighton, who also refused to testify. The bench was told that when first arrested he had admitted knowing Campbell but had denied any charges of theft. When charged he had declared, 'There is always a hope until the court.'

Amongst the other accused were a Mr Arthur Clellingworth, a quarryman who also owned a fried fish shop. He claimed that he had only bought petrol on one occasion, when he needed some for a potato washing machine which he used at his shop. One of the two main customers was alleged to have been a local farmer, Mr George Thomas Thompson of Cragend, who, the police testified, had bought and resold approximately fifty gallons from William Thompson with the two men meeting regularly in the car park of a Rothbury public house to exchange the goods. It was alleged that Thompson was paying 2/6 per gallon but under cross-examination he stated that he had bought no more than eighteen gallons. He had done so only because he had been short for his business and had 'yielded to temptation'.[117]

The other main customer to be brought before the bench was Henry Arkle, a farmer from South Healey Farm, Netherwitton, whom the police alleged had confessed to receiving approximately forty gallons from William Thompson. He used to visit Mr Thompson's house to collect the fuel but before the bench would only admit to having received some eight to ten gallons for which he paid 2/6 per gallon. The cases were adjourned until the November hearings after a request from the solicitor acting for several of the defendants, Mr Wade.

Others to be accused were: George E. Renwick, farmer, of Canada Farm, Longframlington; Alf S. Stephenson, farmer, Blagdon Burn Farm, Longframlington; Alfred Rowe, blacksmith, North Shields; James E. Gibson, sawyer, Blyth; George Forster Cairns, farmer, High Weldon Farm, Longframlington; Ivor William Hutton, gamekeeper, West Lodge, Nunnykirk, Netherwitton; and Peter Aitchison, farmer, Morrelhirst Farm, Longframlington.

The Northumberland Quarter Sessions held in early October duly heard the cases of Sanderson, Campbell, Creighton, Clellingworth and William Thompson (all pleaded guilty except Creighton). Clellingworth and Thompson were both bound over by the bench but the others were more harshly dealt with. John Campbell (45) was bound over on the charges of receiving stolen petrol but was fined £25 for acquiring petrol without a licence. Both the drivers, Sanderson and Creighton, were charged with having stolen the petrol from their employer, acquiring petrol without a licence and furnishing petrol to others. Reflecting the seriousness of the offences the two men were sentenced to three months' hard labour. Judge T. Richardson stated that in the future 'other such cases which came before the sessions would be dealt with in a very different way'.[118]

In November the bench heard more evidence and quickly found the remainder of those charged with receiving guilty and fined each the sum of £2 plus £2 2s in costs. However, the case had turned up new evidence which seemed to hint at an even deeper conspiracy and the manager of the quarry, George Norman Smith, and the director of the Ewesley Quarry Company, William Emans, were both summonsed to appear charged with failing to keep a record of their petrol supplies, failing to deliver coupons to the proper authorities in a timely manner and aiding and abetting with the theft of petrol by their employees. The prosecution outlined just how seriously the alleged crimes were to be taken and pointed out that Inspector Dodds of the Ministry of Fuel and Power stated that in July 1942 he had visited the quarry and ascertained that 792 gallons of petrol had been issued to the company and none had been accounted for and that 'one hundred and sixty two units had not been used and not one of these gallons had been surrendered, leaving 630 gallons unaccounted'. Inspector Dodds went on that in the view of his ministry this was 'an exceedingly grave case'.

The prosecution stated that although there was no evidence that any of the unaccounted for petrol which had been issued to the quarry company had been resold the lax keeping of records and attitudes towards the consumption of petrol meant that both Mr Smith and Mr Emans were both ultimately accountable for the offences. The defence, while pleading guilty, argued that the cases were 'two trumpery charges magnified into twelve and savouring more of persecution than prosecution'.[119] The bench, impressed no doubt by the arguments of the Ministry officials as to the seriousness of the crimes and also of the current shortages of petrol, wasted little time in finding both defendants guilty. Mr Smith was fined £100 (over £4,000 today), Mr Emans £40 and the company itself £20 with 20 guineas costs. In total the sum of fines resulting from the case came to over £181 (almost £7,500 today).

Other crimes heard in November included another case of illegal poaching of salmon from the River Coquet. The accused was a local man, Mr C.F. Wright an engineer from Church House, Rothbury, and the bailiffs argued that he had been caught trying to 'snatch' fish with a gaff from the lower part of Thrum Dam in his hometown. The authorities were keen to point out that the use of gaffs often wounded fish and could lead to the spread of disease with devastating consequences. The lower part of the dam was a bottleneck when salmon were running and any sort of fishing, even with the rod and fly, was forbidden. Although he did not appear, Mr Wright pleaded guilty to the charge and was duly fined £5.

Two more cases heard at the time highlight just how much civil liberties had been eroded by wartime orders. The first involved a canteen worker, Eleanor J. Milburn of 1 Model Cottages, Rothbury, who was charged with failure to comply to a direction from the National Service Officer (it was the role of the National Service Officer to direct workers into jobs where they would be of use to the war effort). Eleanor had been ordered to take up work at a canteen in

Coventry. Faced with prosecution and possible imprisonment the accused agreed to take up the position and the case was adjourned.

The second case involved a young widow, Emma Bachinan from Longframlington, who was accused by the National Service Officer of having left employment without his permission. Mrs Bachinan and her sister had worked at a NAAFI canteen before finding similar work at an aircraft factory. After a period they requested to be allowed to work on the factory floor and were subsequently trained and employed but Eleanor could not be employed in the department she wished to be and subsequently stated her desire to serve abroad. Due to labour shortages this request was denied but Eleanor simply left the factory and returned home to take care of her elderly mother who was ill; she was fined £1.

These were two cases among many similar examples. With the conversion of British society to a total war economy it became essential to call up more workers and to have more centralised governmental power to direct those workers into those areas which were deemed vital to the national war effort. The call up of women was particularly important as they were largely an untapped source of industrial labour. By mid-January the age of women eligible for call-up had been lowered to 19 and many young Northumbrian women found themselves directed to wartime work in munitions and aircraft factories as well as on the land in agriculture and forestry.

As well as contributing to the industry of the country many women had of course already volunteered to serve in the women's branches of the services. One of the first WAAF non-commissioned officers to be posted for service abroad included a Belford woman whose family had a fine service record. Corporal Anne Falla was posted to the Middle East after serving for the last two years in Britain. From Belford, Anne had previously been the manageress of Alnmouth Golf Club but after part of the course was ploughed up she decided that she would resign and serve her country by joining the WAAF. Anne had a sister who was also in the WAAF, serving in Britain, and a brother who was in the Royal Northumberland Fusiliers who had been taken prisoner at Singapore.

One of the outcomes of more people from rural north Northumberland working in more urban areas such as Newcastle was the requirement for more transport links between the city and the country. In August, for example, it was agreed that the Glendale area would receive an additional three buses for use on the Newcastle–Wooler route to help those who were now working regularly in Newcastle.

As we have already seen, petty crime (what would now be termed anti-social behaviour) involving young adults and juveniles had increased. It remained a constant source of concern and a typical case was heard in November when four Thropton teenagers were accused of causing damage worth over £12 to a local doctor's car. The car had been left parked outside a garage in the village but the four had broken into it and smashed two windows, damaged the 'driving gear' and the sliding roof. One of the four, John Saggers (18), tried to take the blame for the others but it quickly became clear that all had participated in damaging the car after drinking. All four defendants (Saggers, Leslie Ross (19), William Shering (17), and

*Corporal Anne Falla served with the WAAF in the Middle East (*Berwickshire News*).*

James Graham Rogerson (19)) were fined £1 and ordered to pay £3 apiece to help cover the cost of repairs.

The scarcity of foodstuffs led some to fall afoul of the law. The pilfering of fruit and vegetables from gardens was increasingly seen as a problem and was treated with harshness by magistrates. At Berwick several offenders had already been fined significant amounts and when two further cases appeared in September the miscreants can surely have expected little sympathy. The first case involved a serving member of the Army, Private Albert Broadfield, who was accused of stealing apples at Longridge Gardens. The police had been informed that fruit was being repeatedly stolen from the garden and a PC hid there to catch any offenders. Private Broadfield confessed to having stolen several apples which he claimed were to eat on a march the next day. He was fined £2.

The next case involved three boys from the Crookham and Cornhill area who were accused of stealing a large number of apples from the Schoolhouse at Cornhill. The boys had waited until the owner of the property was away before raiding his orchard but were subsequently apprehended by the police. One of the boys (James Norman Murray) pleaded guilty and said in evidence that the other two (John Alexander Middlemiss and an unnamed 16-year-old boy), who pleaded innocent, were with him at the time. Despite protestations of innocence from two of the defendants, one of whom claimed to have found fifty apples on the floor of a hut while at a dance, all three were found guilty and fined. Murray was fined £6 and the other two £4 apiece with costs of 9s 4d each.

As we have seen, rationing continued to be a serious concern for many housewives throughout the year and a growing attitude of creatively 'making do' with what could be gathered continued to develop. Demonstrations of recipes using available vegetables, usually those which could be grown at home, at both a national and local level were commonplace. The national demonstrations filtered down to a local level with recipes being given in the local press. At the end of April, for example, the readers of the *Berwick Advertiser* were given three recipes which had recently been demonstrated at a show in London. The recipes included leek pudding served with gravy or cheese sauce,[120] vegetable hot-pot made with leeks (or onions), carrots, turnips and potatoes,[121] and a dish called spring victory which consisted of carrot, turnip, swede, spring onions and powdered egg served with a white sauce.[122]

*Fray Bentos advert encouraging people to make food go further (*Berwickshire News*).*

Manufacturers of tinned goods got in on the act by placing adverts in the press which attempted to give readers (and potential customers) new methods of serving their products. In June the firm of Fray Bentos placed adverts in the Northumberland press which included recipes for corned beef pie[123] and corned beef turnover.[124]

The passion (and necessity) for growing vegetables at home blossomed amongst the population of Northumberland, many of whom had already grown vegetables before the war. Although vegetables were grown as vital food supplies, people also ensured that they had some fun and competitiveness. The network of local horticultural societies in north Northumberland organised annual shows of vegetables and used the opportunities provided by these to raise funds for the war effort. In August the Berwick & District Horticultural Society held its annual show at the RC school in Tweedmouth with all proceeds, primarily from refreshments and the subsequent sale of flowers and vegetables, going to the Red Cross.

The Red Cross continued to be a popular charitable cause throughout the war with many who had people serving in the forces being particularly eager to contribute. Even conscientious objectors could contribute to what was a non-military organisation dedicated to the saving of life. Many people also wanted to see to what uses their donations were being put and to that end the Red Cross Agricultural Fund Mobile Display Unit mounted an extensive tour of Northumberland with events held at Wooler, Belford, Bamburgh, Seahouses and North Sunderland, and Berwick-upon-Tweed.

*Red Cross Agricultural Fund Mobile Display Unit (*Berwick Advertiser*).*

Fish continued to be popular but with the decline in the number of fishing boats (with many trawlermen having gone off to serve with the Royal Naval Reserve or other forces) and growing control of some prices there were, at times, shortages. The fishery officer of the Northumberland Sea Fisheries Committee reported in April that the controlled prices for large haddock and sprags were too low (indeed he claimed that it was at the same level as small whitings and codlings) and that, as these fish were only found in the outer fishing grounds with deeper water, fishermen were reluctant to take the extra risks for such low prices when they could catch codling and whiting in inner grounds for less risk. This had led to a denuding of supplies of fish in the inner grounds and explained the lack of large haddock. Fishery Officer Douglas reported that the situation was such that not one haddock had been landed at Seahouses from December to the end of February. He also stated that if the government had fixed the prices so that large haddock were 1s more than codling and so on the situation would be reversed. He also criticised the price fixing system as it took no account of the quality of the catch, stating that in peace time large haddock at Seahouses usually fetched no less than 8s per stone.

The fishery officer could report better news of the crab and lobster fishing which provided a mainstay to many north Northumberland fishermen. Catches had been good and had recently begun improving in quality too, although he criticised some of the fishermen who packed their crabs at sea and alleged that some were in the practice of including 'all sorts of rubbish … just to get more weight'.[125] Such allegations were at times proven correct and it seems clear that some fishermen were determined to make as large a profit as possible even if it meant cheating the public at a time of national crisis. This further deepened the simmering resentment which was commonplace between those fishermen who were serving in the forces and those who had elected to stay in the industry and make large profits from the inflated prices (obviously this was before the government imposed price restrictions and controls).

As clothing and materials were also in short supply, newspapers encouraged people to make their own clothing. In August young women in the Berwick area were given advice on how to create a dress said to be 'eminently suitable for the younger generation',[126] using a dark and light spotted material. Such articles were run in a regular column entitled 'Home Corner' which charged 8d for paper copies of the patterns along with 8 penny stamps.

One item in short supply was paper and a number of committees and organisations attempted to salvage waste paper so that it could be reused. At the end of July Alnwick Rural District Council heard that, as part of the Northumberland & Durham Book Drive which was being held by all local schools one village school had excelled. The small village of Rennington had initially set the target of 423 books but as of the end of July the school had in fact collected a total of 2,520 books.

Markets continued to operate throughout the war but an ever-growing list of regulations and fixed or controlled prices did stifle the markets and attendances tended to be lower than in pre-war years. In early August Berwick's cattle market had 118 cattle

Dress design patterns were part of the campaign to make do and mend (Berwick Advertiser*).*

available for sale. There was a fair demand for the beasts with black-polled bullocks fetching up to £34 and coloured polled bullocks between £33 and £36.

The trade in the markets fluctuated according to the time of the year and local conditions and in early September Wooler Mart reported that their lamb sales had been a great success with over 2,700 head sold and 'outstanding size and quality' in all categories.[127] Despite some adverse reports in other parts of the county Wooler could report a sustained demand which grew as the sale continued and resulted in prices far exceeding those of last year.

Many livestock farmers in Northumberland, especially those who lived in the hilly areas of the county, were complaining that although price controls had ensured that lowland farmers were making substantial profits it was far more difficult for the hill farmer who had to depend largely on sheep and was affected far more by the vagaries of the weather. To this end the government introduced the Hill Sheep and Hill Cattle Grazing Scheme which had three main aims: to financially help the hill farmer; to preserve the breeding flocks of mountain and hill sheep; and to make fuller use of hill land for the national interest. However, many Northumberland farmers who thought of themselves as hill farmers and who did indeed occupy poor land were angered to find that they were being excluded on the grounds that they were not above 800 metres.

The town's corn market had very small supplies, small to average attendances (possibly due to the holiday weekend) and all prices were at the controlled levels. Of the three suppliers in attendance, Messrs H.O Short & Son reported small demand and did not list prices while the other two suppliers, Messrs H.G. McCreath & Sons Ltd and Messrs Johnson & Darlings Ltd, reported average attendances.

Controlled Prices at Berwick Corn Market, August 1943	
Commodity	**Price (per cwt)**
Barley	26/3 – 27/6
Oats	14s – 14/9
Wheat	14/6

Given the necessity of maintaining and indeed increasing the nation's food supply it came as no surprise that the number of agricultural workers who had been recruited in Northumberland caused a situation on rural housing supplies. National government recognised the problem and agreed to give money to local authorities who would be expected to put out tenders after determining the needs in their areas. Alnwick RDC assessed that a further twenty-two houses would be required along with some improvements to the sewage system at Lesbury. At a meeting of the council it was agreed that four houses would be built at Acklington (at a cost of £3,720), four at Embleton (£3,720), four at Glanton (£3,720), four at Lesbury (£3,720), six at Shilbottle (£5,430 5s) and a new sewer at Lesbury (£30). This amounted to a total of £20,340 (or, today, £836,564) and the council agreed that the government would contribute £12 per year per property over the course of forty years.

Shortages of farm labour were to some extent mitigated by the Land Army, but there were still a great many advertisements in local newspapers for agricultural workers of all types. For example, in January the *Newcastle Journal* contained lengthy sections of positions. The 22 January edition had 115 advertisements for agricultural positions which varied widely and included: a byreman (with an accompanying woman) to milk cows at Brandon White House, Powburn; an elderly man or lad or woman wanted for general farm work and byre work at Bickerton, Thropton; a tractor man, two horsemen and a woman worker for a farm at East Fenton, Wooler; and a steward, a tractor man, two horsemen, a boy and a woman to work in the house at Windy Law, Chathill.

Given the food shortages many Northumbrian housewives looked on Christmas with some concern as they were anxious to provide some semblance of the usual Christmas feast but knew that under the circumstances it might prove difficult. Once more the local press attempted to provide some solutions and the day before Christmas Eve the *Berwick Advertiser* included a column, under the headline 'Of Interest to Women',[128] giving guidance on preparing a Christmas or New Year meal with only limited cooking equipment or a coal fire. The suggested menu included a course of stuffed veal or other meat served with boiled root vegetables, potatoes, steamed sprouts and gravy followed by Christmas pudding with custard. The column gave a timeline of tasks to follow so that dinner would be ready by 1 pm.

Although the wartime farming community of north Northumberland was extremely busy throughout the war they still managed to find time for several traditional pursuits and competitions. Ploughing competitions were still held annually, organised by the Northumberland War Agricultural Committee. At the end of October the annual ploughing and hedgelaying competition was held at Demesne Farm, Thropton, and attracted crowds and a large number of contestants. There were three classes within the competition: ploughing with horse, tractor ploughing and hedgelaying. The assembled farmers were also given a talk by the chairman of the War Ag, Major Rea, on the work being done by the committee and its future intentions. The winners of the competition were Mr J. Gibson of Widdrington (horse ploughing),

Mr J. Young of Silverdale of Thropton (tractor ploughing), and Mr G. Young of Tritlington (hedgelaying). Competitions like these were a great boost to wartime morale within the farming community but also served to educate farmers on new techniques and technologies which were impacting on their industry at the time.

A concern to the authorities was the possibility of declining moral standards amongst young people (especially women). To combat this, various local committees were set up, often with church involvement, and one of the most successful throughout north Northumberland was the Berwick Moral Welfare Committee which, in December, lost its chief worker when Miss A. Leach was ordered to rest by her doctor. A meeting held at the vicarage praised the efforts of Miss Leach who had travelled throughout the north Northumberland area in pursuance of her duties and had had significant success in reaching the young people of the area.

After the Dieppe raid in 1942, Allied commandos did not have the manpower or time to monitor prisoners and many of the Germans who were initially taken prisoner were left tied up. Hitler responded by ordering that all British PoWs be shackled. The Red Cross managed to ensure that only a limited number were shackled (and eventually negotiated an end to the practice) but for a substantial period many British prisoners found themselves bound and ill-treated by their captors.[129] Amongst those who had been shackled was the 28-year-old Viscount Brackley. The viscount was the son of the Earl of Ellesmere but had extensive connections with Northumberland as he was married to the youngest daughter of the Duke of Northumberland and had been taken prisoner while fighting in the retreat to Dunkirk with the Lothian and Border Yeomanry. Brackley had volunteered to be shackled in place of a fellow officer whose health was failing; the local press reported that he had endured 'this Nazi method of ill-treatment' for almost five months.[130]

In the spirit of wartime patriotism and after the 8th Army's recent victory at El Alamein, St. George's Day witnessed a very well attended parade of the Berwick Home Guard and the Royal Northumberland Fusiliers Cadets. The men and boys, with red and white roses in their headgear, marched through the town accompanied by the band of the KOSB to the parish church. The church service was also well attended with guests including the Mayor, the Sheriff, Major Lord Joicey and

Lady Joicey, the Honourable Mrs Bridgeman and Lady Goodson. The military was represented by Captain Sir Edward Blake (Adjutant of the Northumberland Home Guard), Major W.H. Young (Adjutant, 1st Northumberland Cadets) and officers from the infantry training centre at the KOSB depot. Patriotic sermons and hymns were the order of the day and a collection was taken up for the Berwick Infirmary. After the service the men paraded and marched from Wallace Green to the drill hall via Marygate. When the men passed the town hall the salute was taken by a trio of Colonels (Lieutenant Colonels Bridgeman, Goodson and Mulligan); the men gave the salute to the tune of *The British Grenadiers*. At the drill hall the men were treated to an address from Lieutenant Colonel the Honourable H.G.O. Bridgeman on the value of tradition in the British foot regiments of the line during which he praised the 8th Army. He concluded by congratulating the men and cadets on their soldierly appearance.

As the threat of a German invasion receded and the plans for an Allied invasion of occupied Europe became more advanced, the airfields of north Northumberland began to play a greater role in training pilots and aircrew. At the forefront of this effort was RAF Milfield which welcomed a new unit in December 1942, becoming operational in 1943. This was No. 1 Specialised Low Attack Instructors School. The school was created in order to train pilots of Hurricanes and, later, Typhoons and Tempests in the methods of delivering low-level rocket, bomb and strafing attacks on enemy positions, armoured units, transports and trains. Undertaking the creation of such a unit was no mean task and required specific expertise. One of the main contributors was Wing Commander Denys Edgar Gillam DSO DFC AFC. A native of Tyneside, the Wing Commander was a pre-war RAF officer who had fought in the Battle of Britain with 616 Squadron destroying at least fifteen enemy aircraft and being shot down on at least two occasions (at one point being picked up from the sea by an air-sea rescue launch). Going on to command 615 Squadron, Gillam, who earned the nickname 'Kill-Em' Gillam, was awarded a bar to his DFC and a DSO for leading the squadron on shipping attacks which destroyed at least eleven enemy vessels.[131]

One of the results of the formation of the school was the need for extra target ranges. This need was quickly remedied by the construction of a new range on Goswick Sands. The range acquired a motley but useful collection of old tanks, motor vehicles and even old double decker buses. All of these targets were to be destroyed using live weaponry by the students of the school and it was a constant process of ensuring that there were sufficient targets available at the range. Target towing facilities were also expanded with two towing sites established out at sea between Holy Island and the Farnes and the Farnes and Dunstanburgh.

While this was going on the work of the established Operational Training Unit went on as normal. 59 OTU trained pilots from all over the world on the Hurricane but was slated to be equipped with the new Typhoon.

The work of training pilots of all nationalities was arduous and dangerous and there were many accidents, both fatal and non-fatal, during the training process. On 14 January a Hurricane I flown by a young Canadian pilot, Flight Sergeant Richard Davies Maynard, RCAF, dived into the ground just north of Acklington; the young Canadian was killed. Two days later a Hurricane X, piloted by Sergeant James Henry Hobbs, caught fire on the approach to Milfield and the aircraft crashed just north of the airfield. Sergeant Hobbs, who was aged 20, lost his life in the crash and was buried in the nearby Kirknewton Churchyard. The month saw two further aircraft written off in crashes, thankfully without fatalities: the first was on the 23rd when another Hurricane I crashed after hitting a tree while on a night approach to Milfield; two days after this an Oxford from the unit hit cables and crash-landed at Easington.

In February there were a further five accidents including three fatalities. The first fatality was 19-year-old Sergeant Murray Allen Dixon, RCAF, who was killed when his Hurricane I crashed near Chillingham while on a training flight. At around 10.45 am Sergeant Dixon was killed when his Hurricane Mk.I (V6989) crashed beside the Till Bridge at New Town Grange, Chillingham. Such was the impact of the crash that the engine of the aircraft was buried to a depth of 15 feet. Sergeant Dixon was the son of Murray Allen Dixon and Christian Viola McLaren Dixon, of Trenton, Ontario, Canada. He was buried with full military honours at Kirknewton in the churchyard of St. Gregory's. The other two fatalities occurred on 22 February when a Miles Master I carrying an instructor and a pupil crashed at Ancroft. The instructor was a very experienced combat pilot who had flown photo-reconnaissance Spitfires and then the twin engine Whirlwind fighter while a flight commander on 137 Squadron. On 31 October this pilot, Flight Lieutenant John Edward Van-Schaik DFM, RAFVR, was shot down into the sea and found himself adrift in his dinghy. After drifting into a minefield he was rescued after five hours in a very tricky operation but died later. Flight Lieutenant Van-Schaik was 21 at the time of his death. The pupil on the flight was 22-year-old Sergeant Harold Henry Gleadall, RAFVR.[132]

There were a further nineteen casualties that year at Milfield. Given that the pilots were training in dangerous ground level attacks and advanced combat tactics and manoeuvring while in formation it is unsurprising that there were losses. On 27 April two Hurricane Is were involved in a mid-air collision over Belford and both pilots (Flying Officer Eric George Louis Thompson, RAFVR, and Flight Sergeant Kenneth Allen Davies, RAFVR) were killed in the subsequent crash.

Throughout this period the skies over north Northumberland were becoming increasingly crowded and this could sometimes lead to tragic accidents such as that suffered on 5 May by Flight Sergeant Henry Anselm de Freitas, RAFVR. Sent up to practise dogfighting tactics, Sergeant de Freitas's Hurricane collided with a Spitfire from nearby RAF Eshott and both aircraft crashed with the loss of their pilots. Demonstrating the international make-up of the wartime RAF and of those based at Milfield, Flight Sergeant de Freitas was a native of Trinidad.

On 16 September there was an unusual incident involving a B17 of the 8th USAAF which ditched off the Farnes. The aircraft, one of 147 sent to bomb targets in France, was named *Old Ironsides* and was part of the contribution from the 502nd Bomb Squadron. Returning low on fuel and unable to make their Suffolk base (they must have been well off course) the pilot, 1st Lieutenant H.O. Nagorka, took the decision to ditch in the North Sea. Although the ten men of the crew survived the ditching, the B17 sank quickly and two of the crew were drowned. The others managed to reach St. Cuthbert's Island and were later rescued. The eight survivors, including the rear gunner who had lost a leg, were taken to Milfield for evacuation south. A B17 from their squadron was dispatched to pick them up but after landing there was some concern that the huge aircraft might be too large to take off from Milfield (whose runways were designed for fighter aircraft). With a little ingenuity the boundary hedge was partially removed, a temporary steel runway extension was erected and the B17 took off safely.

Although casualties at the OTU and Low Attack School were high, the units were efficient and maintained a high degree of success. By the end of the year 59 OTU had managed to train over 1,200 pilots and the school had produced leaders and attack pilots of a high standard through constantly learning lessons from the results of their ground attack sorties. However, changes were ahead in the next year for RAF Milfield as preparations for the invasion of occupied Europe gathered pace. The new year would see the closure of both 59 OTU and the Low Attack School with both units becoming the first Fighter Leader's School (FLS) which would take on the responsibility of training almost all ground attack pilots.

It was not only Allied aircrew who suffered accidents while flying over Northumberland. On the night of 24/25 March no fewer than eight Luftwaffe bombers crashed in the county. The majority of them flew into hillsides, although some had suffered damage previously. The aircraft were three Dornier 217s and five Junkers JU88s, one of which flew into a hill at Linhope Rigg with the death of its entire crew. At Madam Law Farm, Kirknewton (where many of Milfield's casualties are buried), a Dornier was shot down by anti-aircraft fire (probably from the airfield defences). The bomber struck the top of the hill and bounced over onto the southern slope catching fire and partially disintegrating as it went. One crewman was found dead in the burnt out wreckage while three other fatalities had been thrown clear in the violent crash.

Several of these accidents involved the new Typhoon aircraft which were delivered from April; the first aircraft to land burst a tyre and was written off in the subsequent crash landing, not an auspicious start. The first fatal accident to involve a Typhoon occurred on 20 May when a flying instructor, 22-year-old Flight Lieutenant Michael Clifford Knight, RAFVR, crashed on take-off in a Typhoon Mk Ib (R8709) after suffering engine failure.

Although there had been a number of deaths through enemy bombing in Northumberland throughout 1943, people were heartened by the news of the bombing efforts of RAF Bomber Command as night by night they took the war to German cities. Bomber Command also undertook a huge campaign of minelaying in order to restrict German naval and merchant traffic. These campaigns, as most were aware, came at a massive cost to the men who flew the bombers.[133] On 1 December this area of the war took a tragic toll in Northumberland when a 75 (New Zealand) Squadron Short Stirling III bomber (EH880) returning from a minelaying sortie off the Danish coast was diverted from its home base at RAF Mepal to RAF Acklington because of poor weather conditions. Attempting to make a landing at an unknown airfield in poor weather with heavy fog the pilot was forced to go around a second time but misjudged his approach and at approximately 10.45 pm hit power lines before crashing into a farmhouse at Cliff House Farm, Togston, destroying the second floor of the house. Five children from the Robson family were killed in the accident. The five were: Sheila (19 months); William Matthew (3); Margery (5); Ethel (7); and Sylvia (9). The children's parents and two friends were downstairs at the time and survived with slight injuries.

One of the guests, Mr James (Jimmy) Rowell, was a local butcher who was at the farm salting bacon. He later said, 'We did not realize what had happened until the house collapsed above our heads. We managed to stand up, bruised and badly dazed, and, looking upward

The Robson children, tragically killed when an RAF bomber crashed into their home.

we saw the sky. Mrs Robson tried to make her way towards the stairs, which had been blown away.'

Of the seven-man crew all but one were killed in the crash.[134] The sole survivor, mid-upper gunner Sergeant Kenneth Hook, RAFVR,[135] was saved by Mr Rowell who commented that his 'wife called my attention to a burning object outside which was moving about. We rushed over and found it was a gunner with his clothes alight. Mr Rowell rolled the airman on the ground to extinguish the burning clothes. Although badly burned, the gunner was alive.'[136]

Although the majority of the Luftwaffe was now involved in a largely defensive battle to combat the Allied bombing campaign, fast fighter-bombers (usually Focke-Wulf 190s) still flew low-level tip and run raids against the south coast. One of the RAF squadrons tasked with intercepting them was 266 (Rhodesia) Squadron. Equipped with the Typhoon, the squadron was one of the few which had an aircraft sufficiently fast and manoeuvrable to intercept the FW-190s. On 26 January one of the pilots, Flying Officer Clive Ronald Murray Bell of 266 Squadron, scored a success when he shot down a FW-190. On 3 February, Bell took off in his Typhoon Ib (R7686) to undertake a similar operational patrol. He failed to return and it would appear that his aircraft crashed into the sea as his body was never recovered.[137] Aged 22, from Berwick-upon-Tweed, he had two brothers who were also in the RAF and his parents' anxiety must have been considerable.

We have already seen how the men of the 9th Battalion, Northumberland Fusiliers, were taken prisoner just days after their arrival at Singapore in 1942. For the remainder of the war the survivors of the battalion were used as forced labour by the Japanese on projects such as the infamous Burma–Siam Railroad and the Bridge over the River Kwai. Mistreated and malnourished, the men suffered from brutality and disease and casualties were very high. Amongst these was Berwick-born Fusilier Alan Burnett (29) who died on 19 July at Tonchan, Siam, and was buried in grave 97 of the camp graveyard by his comrades led by a Major Swanton of the Royal Field Artillery. After the war his grave, along with others who died during this monstrous project, was moved to the Kanchanaburi War Cemetery in Thailand.

Another to die a prisoner of the Japanese was Fusilier Wilfred Y. Douglas of 3 Broom Street, Amble. Fusilier Douglas died of dysentery on 11 August at Sunkrae on the Burma/Siam border aged 22 and is now buried at the Thanbyuzayat War Cemetery in Burma, now known as Myanmar. Thanbyuzayat was used as a base hospital for the sick from January to June 1943 but after bombing from the Allies (the camp was next to marshalling yards) the sick were marched to other camps. After the war all graves from the northern section of the railway were transferred here.

As the Battle of Berlin intensified the casualties amongst the men of RAF Bomber Command became critical. Although the bombers were sent out time and again against Berlin it was necessary to vary targets so that the Nazis would not be able to concentrate their defences. On the afternoon of 20 December the men of Bomber Command were summoned for yet another briefing. This time they were being sent to bomb the city of Frankfurt; another tricky target. Amongst the crews who were preparing for the off was that of Flight Sergeant Robert Fiddes of 102 (Ceylon) Squadron. The flight to Frankfurt was a long one and Fiddes and his crew took off from Pocklington at 5.01 pm in Halifax II DY-R

*Flight Sergeant Robert Fiddes, one of many RAF Bomber Command casualties from Northumberland (*Berwickshire News).

A Halifax II similar to the type in which Flight Sergeant Fiddes lost his life (Public Domain).

(JD467); they never returned. Of the seven-man crew, the two gunners survived to become prisoners of war but the other five men, including Berwick-born Flight Sergeant Fiddes, were killed and buried together at Rheinburg War Cemetery.[138]

During this period it was becoming increasingly clear that the tide of the war was beginning to turn in the direction of the Allies and an invasion of occupied Europe appeared increasingly likely. A large number of troops were now based in the county and keeping them entertained was a growing priority. Many of these entertainments were locally organised affairs but ENSA (the Entertainments National Service Association) also played a role. At the end of August the BBC television artist Francis Redvers appeared at Archbold Hall in Wooler with his miniature theatre and cabaret. Mr Redvers wrote the performances, painted the scenery, constructed and controlled the marionettes and spoke all of the dialogue. This was his 810th appearance in front of the troops.

CHAPTER SIX

1944

The Beginning of the End

Of great concern to the authorities were the growing numbers of children born out of wedlock and of venereal disease, especially in areas which hosted members of the forces. Although a number of propaganda campaigns were launched to try to prevent women from entering into casual liaisons (it was still usually seen as being the woman's fault) a radio broadcast on the BBC in March did raise some eyebrows. The topic was part of the *To Start You Thinking* series hosted by Dr Charles Hill and was described in the press as the 'frankest sex broadcast' in which 'nothing was barred' and as a 'free-for-all discussion – one of the frankest ever put on air by the BBC'. Taking part in the debate were Dr Hill and eight men and women aged between 16 and 19 from all over the country (including two, Robert Wheatley and Denise Ingram, from Northumberland); they were described in the press as 'sex crusaders'. The discussion was indeed, by the standards of the time, frank and covered subjects such as how youngsters were educated about sex, what could be done in the future to ensure that knowledge was gained earlier and disseminated more widely, the morality of sex before marriage, and the government's anti-VD campaigns (all of which they supported). One of the 'crusaders' said that they would be hosting a debate back home at their place of work when they returned. They described themselves as crusaders who were campaigning for sex education to be formalised in the British school system from the age of 10 upwards.

One of the Northumbrians, 18-year-old Denise Ingram, described how she had had the facts of life told to her by her mother when she 'was thirteen or fourteen [but she thought] children should be taught at a much younger age than that – ten or even younger'. Showing how

The 'sex crusaders': far left, Robert Wheatley (Northumberland); far right, Denise Ingram (Northumberland) (Daily Mirror).

the young women in particular seemed to believe that they were the issue, one commented that before they went out with a boy young women should know 'all about this power we have to stir him emotionally'. Dr Hill concurred and said that many girls were unaware of the power they had over men, that they 'lead them on and they are surprised at the extent to which they have led them on'.[139]

It was not only the menfolk of Northumberland who were losing their lives in military service, many Northumbrian women found themselves on the front lines during the war. Amongst the female casualties from Northumberland were several nurses. One of these, 32-year-old Sister Sarah Elizabeth Dixon of East Ditchburn, Eglingham, was a member of the Queen Alexandra's Imperial Nursing Service (Reserve) serving aboard the hospital ship HMHS *St. David*. Although the targeting of hospital ships was a war crime and the vessel was well marked, being painted white with illuminated red crosses, the *St. David* was attacked by enemy bombers off Anzio on 24 January 1944. The ship was struck by at least three bombs and sank within five minutes. The crew attempted to save the wounded and 159 people were rescued but 22 passengers, 22 medical staff, the master and twelve crew lost their lives. Amongst the nursing staff to be lost was Sister Dixon. Elizabeth, or Bessie as she was known, had trained as a nurse at Royal Victoria Infirmary in Newcastle and had volunteered for service at the outbreak of war. Having been posted to several shore-based hospitals, she had worked on board the *St. David* since May 1943. It was reported that after the bombs had hit, both Bessie and her colleague, Sister Harrison, had remained on board to aid the wounded.

Relatively minor crimes continued to be heard by magistrates throughout north Northumberland. At Rothbury in May an unfortunate case was heard involving a man who had served with distinction in the last war and had tried to join up in the present war. John Osbourne McDonald of Hartburn was employed at Ewesley Quarry where for some three years he had run a lottery, based on football teams reaching eleven points, amongst his colleagues. In the last few months the lottery had expanded to 105 members and in March two members should have been paid winnings of £10. Mr McDonald failed to make the payments and immediately turned himself into the police saying it was a prosecution case. He confessed that he had illegally taken ten per cent for himself and that on a Saturday night had gone into Rothbury with the money in his wallet but had 'got rather muddled with drink and on the Sunday morning found he had only a few shillings';[140] he immediately telephoned the police to confess. The magistrates heard how Mr McDonald was an educated man, an engineer, but was something of a wanderer, that he was previously of good character but had fallen afoul of excess drink. Taking all of these things into account the magistrates agreed to waive any prison sentence and bound Mr McDonald over for the sum of £5 adding that they hoped he would not appear before them again.

At the same hearing, Thropton physician Dr Rosa Salome Pelly was charged with having left her motor car with its engine running and its handbrake off. The car had been observed by Auxiliary Policewoman Elsie Bamborough rolling across the main road unattended before colliding with a house wall in Front Street, Rothbury. Policewoman Bamborough turned off the engine and removed the keys before fetching Dr Pelly who had gone into a house. Sergeant Bell quickly arrived on the scene and questioned Dr Pelly who admitted that she had failed to apply the handbrake but denied that the engine was running; Dr Pelly claimed she had rushed inside to get some petrol coupons. Dr Pelly claimed at the trial that, although she admitted not applying the handbrake and not possessing a current driving licence (it had expired in January), she was sure that the engine had not been started by her; she was not denying the charges but was pleading only in the interest of truth. The magistrates found Dr Pelly guilty and fined her £2 with a further fine of 10s for the licencing offence.

Despite the ongoing background of the war the members of

Rothbury Rural District Council met in April to discuss a disgraceful set of earth closets at several properties in Longframlington. Dr Hedley, the medical officer, had inspected the site and described them as 'not only a disgrace but a danger in hot weather' with Councillor Cowens stating that they were only 'cleaned out once in probably twelve or fifteen months … they were full of ashes to the top and the ashes were running over the cement almost to the back doors'.[141] The sanitary inspector informed the council that the contractor who was supposed to empty the privies seldom performed his duties and that, despite the residents being willing to pay, the council could not find anyone else due to the war. He also explained how they had planned to install water flush toilets but the war had intervened and it was unlikely they would now be able to do so until after the war. This was not an isolated case (although it was the worst) in the area as there were similar privies in Rothbury as well as others in Longframlington. The need for flush toilets was pushed by Councillor Brown who explained how he had spoken with the man contracted to empty the privies at Rothbury and how he had described the work as being extremely unpleasant. However, Councillor Hills took a rather more phlegmatic attitude when he stated that as the problem had existed for twenty years or more it would no doubt have to go on now until after the war. The sanitary inspector did agree to talk to the contractor and see if some solution could be arrived at.

The sanitary problems plaguing the Rothbury district were not isolated. In June, Amble Urban Council met to discuss post-war development and amongst the foremost issues was the establishment of a water carriage system and the installation of water flush toilets to replace earth closets. The council also had plans to build 200 new houses in Amble with the first 50 being constructed in the first year after the war, and it was keen to concentrate the new houses in two new developments instead of scattering them around the area.

The council also had ambitious plans to develop the fishing industry in the town as it did not expect the government to assign any light industry to the area. It recognised that there would be a need to consult with the fishermen themselves before finalising any plans but hoped that improvements to the facilities for landing catches would enable the industry to grow fourfold in the post-war years. Councillor Anderson expressed the view that in order for this development to succeed it would be vital to consult with the deep-sea fishermen as they would form the backbone of any post-war improvement, but he was afraid that they would not be interested unless a better, non-tidal, harbour could be provided (a vast undertaking). The chairman answered saying that it was the intention to encourage not only the deep-sea fishermen but also the herring boats and the Icelandic boats to dock at Amble. It was agreed that a round-table meeting would be held between the council and the fishermen to discuss possible plans and ways of moving forward.

The council was also pleased to announce that in view of its good financial state it was able to donate £500 to the Alnwick 'Salute the Soldier' Week and proud that this was the first time that Amble UC had been able to donate money in this way.

With food supplies continuing to be a concern the popularity of small pig clubs continued to soar. In May it was decided to place the Warkworth and District Pig Club under the chairmanship of a local county councillor, Captain G. Tate. The inaugural address was given by the regional officer of the Small Pig Keepers Council, Mr A.M. Briggs, on the management of pig clubs and on the advantages of forming and running such a club. The second speaker, Mr W.L. Oliver of Morpeth, was keen to explain the strategy of pig feeding and the uses of different foodstuffs in producing pigs.

In June the growing need for an increase in the breeding of cattle for beef was highlighted at a livestock demonstration in Rothbury. The event, held by the War Ag at Rothbury Auction Mart, attracted a large crowd of farmers from across Northumberland. Speakers included the chair of the War Ag, Professor R.W. Wheldon, and veterinary surgeon Mr W. Lyle Stewart, both of King's College (now Newcastle University), and the County War Executive Officer (Mr E. David).

Professor Wheldon said in his address that the days of Northumberland largely depending on imported store cattle for feeding up were ending and that in the future the number of home-bred beasts would need to increase significantly. Stores would need to be improved if this was the case despite the expertise of the Northumberland farmer in producing grass-fed cattle not being 'excelled in any part of the country'.[142] Professor Wheldon also pointed out that demand for sheep would also increase but, as Northumberland was a prime producer of both high quality mutton and sheep for breeding for export elsewhere, the county was well placed to take advantage of any future increase in demand.

Because of the build-up to D-Day, the activities at the training airfields in north Northumberland stepped up a pace, most notably at RAF Milfield; once again, the training process was not without its own tragedies which often brought the war home to the people of this rural area. Having seen previously the international make-up of the aircrew at RAF Milfield we should not be surprised to find there was another Trinidadian casualty, Flying Officer Leslie Look-Yan. It would appear that he may have been at least partially the victim of wartime training oversights as it seems he had spent a great deal of his service training glider pilots in Tiger Moth aircraft. Although he would have thus racked up an impressive amount of flying time most of this would have been with a glider pilot actually doing the flying. Posted to Milfield without any conversion period on the Hurricane, Look-Yan's first flight in the more powerful aircraft was disastrous. The unfortunate flying officer barely got off the ground before crashing; but he was unhurt and was sent off again. His subsequent flights must have convinced the instructors that he could indeed fly the Miles Master and the Hurricane but it seems they were wrong. The 21-year-old flying officer was killed in a Hurricane IIb (Z3076) on 14 January. He was practising low-level flying when the propeller of his aircraft struck the ground and he crashed through a hedge into some trees at Rosedean Farm, Wooperton.

Yet another casualty of flight training was Flight Sub-Lieutenant (Acting) John William Pollock (Jack) Mabon of Chirnside. Jack was based at HMS *Jackdaw* (RNAS Crail), a base which trained torpedo bomber pilots and crews, when he lost his life in a flying accident on 19 October. The 19-year-old's body was brought back to his home village for burial at Chirnside Parish Churchyard. Tragically Jack's 28-year-old brother Adam had been killed on operations just four months previously. Pilot Officer Adam Mabon was a flight engineer in a 408 (RCAF) Squadron Lancaster BII which was lost on 13 June while attacking Cambrai in support of the attempts to break out from the Normandy beachheads.[143]

As minds turned to the forthcoming invasion of Europe, the fighting in Italy was also continuing with severe casualties. Rachel Wilkinson, the wife of Fusilier David Wilkinson, received word that her husband had been reported missing in the fighting around Cassino in February. The Allies had made a landing behind the Anzio line in January in order to force a breakthrough but the fighting was so severe that it was not until May that Cassino actually fell. It was later confirmed that Fusilier David Turnbull Wilkinson, 2nd Battalion, Royal Scots Fusiliers, had been killed in action on 1 February aged 33. A Milfield man, Fusilier Turnbull left behind his wife and his parents William and Elizabeth, who lived at Council Houses, Milfield.

*Flight Sub-Lieutenant (Acting) John William Pollock 'Jack' Mabon of Chirnside was killed in a flying accident (*Berwick Advertiser*).*

RAF Bomber Command had continued its campaign against the German capital throughout the winter of 1943 and 1944 at great cost in lives to the airmen involved. Many of these men came from Northumberland. Sergeant James E. Johnston of the Parochial Hall, Berwick-upon-Tweed, had volunteered for aircrew duties and was trained as a wireless operator/air gunner before being assigned to 78 Squadron at Breighton. On the night of 24/25 March he was bound for Berlin with the rest of his crew in Halifax III (HX355, EY-D). Near the target zone the Halifax was attacked and badly damaged by a night fighter and although the crew attempted to return to base the damage proved to be too severe and the aircraft was abandoned near the Dutch coast. All seven of the crew, including Sergeant Johnston, were taken prisoner and spent the rest of the war in a variety of prison camps.[144]

The preparations for D-Day were not without loss as the Allied air forces attempted to pummel German coastal defences. As the Allies began routinely to mount attacks on occupied Europe in the preparatory build-up to an invasion, losses amongst RAF fighter-bomber squadrons increased. Another Northumbrian fighter-bomber pilot to lose his life in such a mission was 21-year-old Flight Lieutenant David Patrick Murray Bell of Highcliffe, Berwick-upon-Tweed. Bell was flying a Typhoon Ib (MN545) of 263 Squadron on 21 May 1944 when he lost his life. He was an experienced airman, having joined the RAF straight after graduating from Repton College. It would appear that his aircraft crashed into the sea as he was initially posted missing and it was not until January 1945 that his death was confirmed. For his parents, Major Ronald P. M. Bell and Mary Bell, the loss must have been appalling as this was the second of three sons in the RAF to lose his life; readers will recall that his older brother was lost, also while flying a Typhoon, in 1943.[145]

In the early hours of D-Day yet another north Northumbrian man serving in the RAF lost his life. Flight Lieutenant Victor George Brewis was a 28-year-old navigator in a Mosquito FB VI of 605 (County of Warwick) Squadron and had been tasked with an intruder mission to seek out and destroy enemy aircraft and airfield facilities. After departing from RAF Manston nothing more was heard and the two-man crew of Mosquito NT122 failed to return. It was subsequently established that the aircraft had crashed into the Ijsselmeer at 2 am and both crewmen had been killed. Flight Lieutenant Brewis was from Wooler and was buried at Hoorn General Cemetery.[146]

In the rush of casualties caused by the D-Day landings the bureaucratic system intended to keep relatives informed sometimes lagged behind events. For some this proved tragic but for Mrs Florence Smith of Hope House, Wooler, there was a happier outcome. Florence received news that her husband Sapper Edwin Smith, RE (attached to the Royal Engineer Tank Corps), had been wounded and swept overboard during the invasion. Thankfully he had been rescued from the sea after over three hours. One can imagine Mrs Smith's happiness when her husband walked through the door of their home a few days later after recovering from his injuries.

With the news of the successful establishment of a beachhead in Normandy the local press, at the instructions of the government, ran campaigns explaining that the subsequent disruption to some passenger railway services was due to the fact that more trains were required by the forces for the purpose of ensuring that reinforcements and supplies were maintained to the beachhead. The Railway Executive Committee ran a series of adverts urging people to remain at home and not to take summer holidays on the trains as track space was required for the movement of men and materiel to the front.

For men from north Northumberland, casualties continued in the fierce fighting in the days and weeks after D-Day. The RAF's Bomber Command continued to support the land forces in a sustained campaign of strategic bombing of communications, transport and airfield facilities. On the night of 7/8 June, bomber formations totalling 192 Halifaxes, 122 Lancasters and 20 Mosquitoes attacked targets at Achères, Juvisy-sur-Orge, Massy-Palaiseau and Versailles, while a force of Lancasters and Mosquitoes (of 1, 5 and 8 Groups) attacked a six-way road junction between Bayeux and Saint-Lô (it was believed that enemy armour units and fuel dumps were in the surrounding woods). Part of the force assigned to attack Juvisy (which contained a rail marshalling yard) was that of Flight Lieutenant D. Davies and crew of 78 Squadron. They had taken off in their Halifax III (LV868) from Breighton and had a relatively quiet trip bombing from 5,000 feet at 1.13 am. However, they were then attacked by a German night fighter which badly damaged the Halifax and the crew were forced to struggle to Britain before making a forced landing at RAF West Malling in Kent at a little before 3 am. Although six of the seven men crew survived the rear gunner, 20-year-old Flight Sergeant Charles William Lillico, died of injuries he had sustained. Flight Sergeant Lillico, who was a member of the RAFVR, was a native of Alnwick where his parents, William Pringle Lillico and Sarah Isabella 'Cissy', received the terrible news at their Greenfield Avenue home. The body of Flight Sergeant Lillico was returned to his family and he was buried in his hometown at a well-attended service on 13 June.

The fighting in Normandy continued to take its toll and on 11 June yet another north Northumberland man lost his life. Twenty-year-old Private Cecil Selby of Whittingham was killed

INVASION

means more trains

for the

Fighting Forces

RAILWAY EXECUTIVE COMMITTEE

*Adverts urged people to curtail their travel arrangements in the wake of D-Day (*Berwick Advertiser*).*

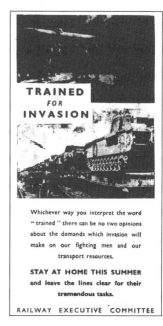

TRAINED
FOR
INVASION

Whichever way you interpret the word "trained" there can be no two opinions about the demands which invasion will make on our fighting men and our transport resources.

STAY AT HOME THIS SUMMER and leave the lines clear for their tremendous tasks.

RAILWAY EXECUTIVE COMMITTEE

*With the increased requirements of supplying troops in Normandy the rail system became overloaded (*Berwick Advertiser*).*

while fighting as part of the 1st King's Own Scottish Borderers (KOSB) just five days after the battalion had landed on 'Queen' Beach on D-Day. Along with many comrades who were killed in this early phase of the fighting Private Selby's body was buried at Ryes War Cemetery, Bazenville.[147]

In August came news of the death of the MP for Berwick. Captain George Charles Grey MP, 4th Battalion, Grenadier Guards, 6th Guards Tank Brigade, was killed on 30 July when a sniper shot him as he advanced with his Churchill VII tank through Lutain Wood near the hamlet of Le Repas some 33 km south-west of Caen.[148] Interestingly Captain Grey's is one of only two individual burials of British soldiers killed during the Second World War and recognised as an isolated grave by the Commonwealth War Graves Commission. Most burials were collected at the end of the war and assembled in nearby war cemeteries, but both Captain Grey's family and the people of Le Repas petitioned strongly for his grave to remain where it had been dug by his men and a private memorial was erected by the family.[149]

As the fighting in Europe continued, the Allies launched a bold plan to cross the Rhine before the German Army could reorganise its lines. The resulting operation was code-named 'Market Garden' but the paratrooper landings to capture river crossings at Arnhem ended in disaster through poor planning, inadequate intelligence and adverse weather conditions. There were large numbers of casualties and prisoners as a result of the operation, several from north Northumberland. Amongst the fatalities was Lance Corporal Thomas John William Bryson, Border Regiment, 1st (Airborne) Battalion. A 28-year-old married man from Tweedmouth, Thomas was killed on the fifth day of the operation, 21 September, and is buried at the Arnhem Oosterbeek War Cemetery. Private Stanley Humpherson, KOSB, a native of Milfield and Company Sergeant Major William Henderson, KOSB, were taken prisoner during the fighting around Arnhem; both men were part of the 1st (Airborne) Battalion.

The bitter fighting as the German Army retreated from Italy also claimed Northumbrian lives. After the fall of Rome in June the Germans retreated to a series of well-prepared defensive lines named Trasimene, Arezzo, Arno and Gothic. The fighting to take the eastern section of the Gothic line was particularly fierce around Montecchio and the surrounding countryside. The combat on the last day of August

CSM William Henderson, taken prisoner at Arnhem (Berwick Advertiser).

Lance Corporal Bryson, killed at Arnhem (Berwick Advertiser).

Pvt Stanley Humpherson was taken prisoner during the fighting around Arnhem (Berwick Advertiser).

claimed the life of 26-year-old Gunner James Nairn, 3rd Medium Regiment, Royal Artillery. James was from Waren Mill, Belford, and the news of his death was delivered there to his parents Robert and Margaret; James is buried in the Montecchio War Cemetery.

As the Allied armies occupied Brussels, documents were captured revealing German plans of a seaborne invasion of Berwick-upon-Tweed. In December the *Berwickshire News* carried an article which stated that the plans were dated 1940 and 1941 and contained detailed maps identifying local landmarks such as the Town Hall, the railway station, bridges and streets. The documents were also claimed to reveal that in the event of capturing the town the German army HQ would be established at the King's Arms Hotel.

We have already seen how dangerous the training of new aircrew could be with many losing their lives in crashes while training over Northumberland. Not all of these men came from Northumbrian bases as

Gunner James Nairn of Belford, killed in the fierce fighting in Italy (Berwick Advertiser).

the county was used extensively by trainee bomber crews from more southerly locations for cross-country training. On 15 October another incident took place when a Halifax V bomber (DK116) from 1667 Heavy Conversion Unit (HCU) crashed near Kielder. 1667 HCU was one of several HCUs operating around the country whose role was to allow trainee aircrew in the final phases of their training to become familiar with the operation of heavy four-engined aircraft. This crew took off from RAF Sandtoft near Scunthorpe for a night cross-country exercise but while over Northumberland at 12,000 feet the port inner engine caught fire. With the pilot, Pilot Officer Herbert George Haddrell, finding it impossible to extinguish the fire he ordered the crew to bail out. Three of the crew immediately complied with the order and left the aircraft but it seems that the rear gunner became trapped in his turret and that two of the remaining crew made frantic efforts to free him while the pilot attempted to keep the aircraft in the air. In a final desperate attempt to extinguish the fire the pilot put the aircraft into a dive hoping, no doubt, that the slipstream would put the fire out but, unfortunately, the Halifax crashed into Caplestone Fell, Glendhu Hill, and the four crew who had remained on board were killed in the impact and fire.[150]

As was so often the case when aircraft crashed in the more remote parts of north Northumberland, the first men on the scene were two local shepherds. One of the men, Adam Steele of Willow Bog Farm, had been visiting a fellow shepherd at High Long House and was walking home accompanied by his friend when they witnessed the crash. Despite the darkness and rough terrain, the two men immediately attempted to reach the site to ascertain if there were any survivors. With the only light coming from a storm lantern and the flames from the crashed bomber the two men reached the sight but discovered that most of the crew had been killed. However they located two of the surviving crew, one of whom had broken his leg. They comforted them until more locals arrived from five miles away to evacuate the men to the road where police and ambulances awaited them.[151]

When the V-weapons began landing on the south of England a further wave of evacuations began with many women and children being sent to the north of England. Many were sent to Northumberland and this new influx was welcomed in much the same positive manner as those earlier in the war had been. Once more, billets were scarce and adverts appeared in the local press asking householders to inform Miss M.F. Charlton of Beech Cottage, Rothbury, if they were willing to house any of the evacuees from London and the South. The evacuees were organised into three categories: unaccompanied schoolchildren; mothers and infant children; and expectant or nursing mothers. Most of these late-war evacuees took an active part in their new foster communities and in August one 15-month-old evacuee won first prize in the Red Cross fete baby show at Alnwick. London-born Janet Marriott-Statham was entered by her mother after her new neighbours persuaded her and swept the board, even making time to make friends with the Duke of Northumberland's puppy!

We have seen how many Northumbrians went on to make a major contribution to the war effort and how some were rewarded for their courage. One such man with extensive Northumberland connections was Squadron Leader Joseph (Joe) Berry who rose to fame during the

Amongst the new wave of evacuees from the south were a large number of women with young children (Berwick Advertiser).

battle to defeat the V-weapons. Indeed, despite the awards of the DFC and two subsequent bars to the medal, there were many who argued that Joe should have received the nation's highest award, the Victoria Cross, for his courageous actions in closing to almost suicidal range in order to shoot down a V-weapon which was heading for the WRAF billets at RAF West Malling.

Joe was born in County Durham before relocating with his family to Stampeth, near Alnwick, from where he attended the Duke's School in Alnwick. While a student he earned a reputation as being bright with a quick mind while also being quiet and unobtrusive of character. Since the age of 12 Joe had been fascinated with flying and had earned a ride in one of the aircraft of Cobham's Flying Circus when the troupe visited Alnwick in 1932. After school Joe found employment in Nottingham where he married a local woman (Joyce) and shortly before the start of the war he volunteered for aircrew service.

After his pilot training Joe was posted to 256 Squadron flying Boulton-Paul Defiant night fighters and quickly earned a reputation as a cool and skilful pilot. The Defiant had originally been designed as a fighter but proved woefully inadequate; after suffering massive losses

A Boulton-Paul Defiant similar to that flown by Squadron Leader Joseph Berry (Public Domain).

during the Battle of Britain it was withdrawn into the role of interim night fighter. The inadequacies of the Defiant almost claimed Joe's life on the night of 4 November 1941 when his engine failed and he and his gunner were forced to bail out. Joe came down safely by parachute but his gunner, Flight Sergeant E.V. Williams, was blown out to sea and drowned (his body being recovered the next morning at Fleetwood).

Bristol Beaufighter similar to that which Squadron Leader Berry flew while stationed in North Africa (Public Domain).

Despite this mishap Joe was commissioned as a pilot officer in March 1942 and posted to Liverpool along with his squadron (which by the end of the year was flying the Bristol Beaufighter, a vast improvement over the Defiant). While the rest of 256 Squadron was sent to Northern Ireland, Joe was kept in England as a night fighter trainer. At the end of January Joe and his new navigator/wireless operator (Ian Watson) were posted to 153 Squadron at Maison-Blanche in North Africa. Joe was once again forced to bail out during his time with 153 Squadron. During the early hours of 11 April 1943, Joe and Ian were returning home when one of their Beaufighter's engines burst into flames and the two parachuted over the Mediterranean. Both crewmen survived the incident despite having to spend over six hours in their dinghy.

Shortly afterwards the pair were posted to 255 Squadron and began flying months of monotonous patrol and convoy escort work until they managed to shoot down a Junkers JU88 in September; this was the first of three victories for the crew (the others were a Messerschmitt ME210 on 10 September and a JU88 on 23 October) before being sent on leave and returned to England. Upon his return Joe undertook work for a top secret unit working on radio countermeasures, radar and other technological innovations.

There followed a period as an instructor, the award of the DFC, and promotion to flight lieutenant. Joe was then posted with a small group of pilots who had experience flying the new Hawker Tempest to a unit designed to tackle the new V-weapons which were raining down on the south of England. Joe shot down his first V-weapon on 28 June and subsequently proved himself an expert at this highly dangerous task. Although the V-weapons had no defensive armament they were very difficult to hit and their warhead packed a potent punch, meaning that an aircraft shooting down a flying bomb was at great risk if it got too close to the blast radius. On the night of 2 July, Joe chased a flying bomb and succeeded in shooting it down but was a little too close and his Tempest was badly damaged by the resulting blast. Joe managed to bring the aircraft back to an airfield and made a skilful landing with no engine. Upon coming to a halt he commented to the ground crew saying, 'That aircraft's unserviceable, Sergeant.'

By mid-July the small unit of which Joe was a founder had lost every member except himself (two had been killed and one injured). On the night of 23 July came the incident for which many thought Joe should have been awarded the VC. Chasing and opening fire on a V-weapon, Joe set it on fire but noticed it was descending towards the buildings surrounding RAF West Malling. He instantly closed to just 100 yards and destroyed the flying bomb. While this undoubtedly saved many lives it also severely damaged Joe's Tempest and he was forced to land the aircraft at almost top speed after its throttle jammed. Met on the tarmac by an ambulance, Joe wryly commented that he would ride in front and asked for 'someone to tow the aircraft off the runaway'. On 4 August Joe was awarded the first bar to his DFC (his commanding officer had in fact twice recommended him for the higher award of a DSO) and the next night he celebrated the award by successfully shooting down five flying bombs! Many on the squadron and in the wider RAF believed the act was worthy of the award of a VC but this was not promulgated.[152] He was promoted to squadron leader and, recognising his expertise, the authorities gave him his own squadron dedicated to the destruction of the flying bomb.

For his newly created squadron (501) Joe recruited experienced night pilots from all over Fighter Command and his success was immediate; just days after taking over command, 501 Squadron shot down eight flying bombs in one night and the successes were to continue. Joe's personal score steadily mounted and he quickly became the acknowledged expert on the aerial interception of flying bombs. Over the weeks and months Joe and his squadron made a huge contribution to the lessening of the threat from the flying bombs, and he was asked to attend a senior level conference on

Squadron Leader Joseph 'Joe' Berry DFC (and two bars) (Public Domain).

the threat. Because of the British successes in destroying flying bombs the Luftwaffe came up with a new plan to launch the bombs from bombers.

Aware of this development, the RAF decided to have 501 Squadron mount reconnaissance and attack missions on the airfields from which these bombers were based. Flying the first of this type of operation,

A Hawker Tempest V similar to that in which Squadron Leader Berry was killed (Public Domain).

Joe's flight encountered bad weather and were forced to turn back; they tried again the next day, 2 October 1944. En route to their target airfield at Zwischenahn in north-western Germany Joe led his aircraft at low level past Veendam. Coming under machine gun fire Joe's aircraft was hit and Joe himself probably wounded. His horrified pilots observed him slumped over his controls but his Tempest, leaking glycol, climbed and they thought that perhaps he was going to bail out only to hear him on RT say, 'Carry on chaps, I've had it.' His aircraft then turned upside down and crashed into farmland, bursting into flames. Joe was posthumously awarded a second bar to his DFC for his courage and skill in shooting down the phenomenal total of fifty-eight flying bombs (all at night) plus the three aircraft in North Africa.[153]

September saw Rothbury Rural District Council joining those local authorities who were already making advanced plans for post-war development. The RDC agreed to a plan to construct sixty-four additional dwellings over two years but, unlike the development at Amble mentioned earlier, these would be scattered around the district, as follows:

Place	Year	Number of Dwellings
Alwinton	1	4
Harbottle	1	4
Longframlington	1	8
Netherton	1	8
Longframlington	2	8
Thropton	2	6
Rothbury	2	26

The medical officer, Dr Hedley, reported that health in the district was as could be expected but that there had been an epidemic of measles which had continued from the previous year. By September there had been 87 cases reported (down on the 180 from the previous year) with the majority coming from Longframlington and Thropton, but only one at Rothbury. Dr Hedley explained that he believed this was because a majority of children in Rothbury had been exposed to the disease in an epidemic in 1940 when there had been 70 cases in the village and that they were now largely immune.

During the first week of October, a WAAF Sergeant cook lost her life after a bicycling accident at Warkworth. Sergeant Jane Grant Beggs (43), who was from Ulster, had been out cycling with two other WAAFs when they came to a steep hill leading down to the bridge at Warkworth. Sergeant Beggs asked the others if she should cycle down as she had no brakes. Her two companions advised her against it and said they would cycle down and wait for her to walk down. However it seems Sergeant Beggs decided to freewheel down but lost control and crashed into the bridge wall. Flung over the parapet she landed on rocks below sustaining several serious injuries including a compound fracture of the elbow and a fractured pelvis. When her companions reached her Sergeant Beggs was conscious but in shock and expressing concerns over how they might get home. After being taken to hospital and treated by an RAF doctor Sergeant Beggs died.

Winter came early in 1944 with reports from Rothbury at the beginning of November that snow had lain on the Cheviot Hills for several days and that the top lake at Cragside had already frozen across. This was far earlier than normal and reports said, 'The Cheviots look like Switzerland.'[154]

Despite this, fundraising attempts continued throughout the county with at least two whist drives and dances being held in November. The first was at Milfield where a great number of prizes were won at the local school and country dances and reels danced with delight by the large attendance; music was supplied by the Wooler band. As the result of such a successful event the Red Cross benefited by the sum of £12 18s 3d. The second event was held at Powburn Village Hall. There was whist, then refreshments served by the Ladies Committee, and a dance with music by Thompson's Band. A dance prize was awarded to Piper and Mrs Armstrong and the following day (a Saturday) another dance was held which was very well attended. The sum of £11 8s 8d was raised by the two events and was donated to the Welcome Home Fund which at this point stood at £135.

A further drive was held at the Reading Room in Doddington for the Welcome Home Fund in early December and this was followed by a whist drive and dance held by Doddington Young Farmer's Club which raised a substantial sum for the club funds. The club alongside

Milfield Young Farmer's Club also arranged an inter-club discussion meeting for 19 December which gave some hint of the amazing technological transformation which the war had brought about in agriculture. The topic for debate was, 'Had the combine harvester come to stay?' with Milfield proposing and Doddington opposing. Further whist drives in December were held at Norham, Tillmouth and Ilderton.

At the end of November, the 1st Battalion Northumberland Home Guard held their stand-down parade and service in Berwick. In the afternoon the various companies arrived by bus and marched separately to the Parish Church where the vicar of Berwick conducted a service. Then the battalion as a whole, accompanied by the band from the Infantry Training Camp, marched through the town to the Corn Exchange where the salute was taken by Colonel Viscount Allendale.

*'F' (Berwick) Company of 1st Northumberland Home Guard. The men were proud to take part in the stand-down parade in November (*Berwick Advertiser*).*

In the build-up to a sixth wartime Christmas the people of the Berwick area enjoyed a large toy fair which was held at the Town Hall. The fair, organised by the Women's Voluntary Service (WVS), was opened by Kathleen, Lady Armstrong, and attracted large crowds, especially of those who had young children. All proceeds went to the Red Cross with over £400 being raised.

On 7th December the children of Holy Island were treated to a Christmas treat when the local church along with volunteers held a tea party and present-giving. A Christmas tree was provided and a Punch and Judy show well received although the car bringing the planned participants in the entertainment party broke down in the poor weather and the rest of the entertainment had to be improvised. The children were presented with more than two presents from the tree by Santa Claus (played by Police Constable Steele) and an apple each while the under-fives also received a doll. Carol singing was performed with gusto and was concluded with the National Anthem. The next day (Sunday) a well-attended children's service was held at the Presbyterian Church and in the evening there was carol singing in one of the islander's homes.

It was not only the men of RAF Bomber Command who were carrying the offensive to Germany. Since 1942 the men of the USAAF had been mounting daylight bombing raids on Germany and occupied Europe. By late 1944 the Luftwaffe was no longer the force that it had been, but many of the raids of the USAAF were still heavily opposed and casualties, sometimes heavy, remained a sad fact of life for the young men who had come from America to carry on the fight from Britain.[155]

On 16 December the crews of the 303rd Bomb Group (Heavy) of the USAAF were briefed for yet another raid on Germany, this time to the marshalling yards at Ulm. Like many raids at this time of year the weather played a hand and, in rapidly deteriorating conditions, the raid was aborted just after 10 am and the aircraft ordered to land at a variety of airfields to limit the risk of collision in the growing storm and blizzard conditions. Amongst the aircraft was B-17G (44-6504) containing the nine-man crew of 2nd Lieutenant George A. Kyle, Jnr. The crew rapidly ran into difficulties as their navigational aids became inoperable. Kyle requested radio bearings on several occasions but was led astray by ghost signals. Although they still had their bombs aboard the crew dared not jettison them as they did not know if they were over a built-up area or not. Left with little choice, Kyle took the decision just after 1 pm to descend to 3,000 feet to try to establish their position. Shortly after doing so, the B-17 struck West Hill at the Cheviot and the aircraft skidded across a peat bog disintegrating as it went. Of the nine-man crew the two in the nose of the aircraft, navigator Flying Officer

The B17 crew of 2nd Lieutenant George A. Kyle Jnr which crashed in the Cheviots (303rd Bomb Group website).

Fred Holcombe, Jnr, and togglier (air bomber) Sergeant Frank R. Turner were killed instantly. All of the remaining crew were injured to some extent with the pilot breaking his jaw and being pulled from the aircraft by his co-pilot Flying Officer James H. Hardy. The three crewmen from the cockpit area (the pilot, co-pilot and the engineer Sergeant Ernest G. Schieferstein) walked from the wreckage which was now on fire, managed to find a farm in the blizzard, and were taken to an RAF first aid station at Berwick-upon-Tweed. In the back of the aircraft the remaining crewmen had minor injuries and several were knocked out by the impact. The radio operator, Sergeant Joel A. Berly, attempted to put out a fire in the bomb bay but became trapped when the fuselage floor collapsed. Waist gunner Sergeant William R. Kaufman recovered consciousness in time to rescue Sergeant Berly and ball turret gunner Sergeant George P. Smith. Once they exited the aircraft they found the dazed rear gunner Sergeant Howard F. Delaney wandering confusedly with a severe head wound. The four men took shelter in a ditch a short distance from the aircraft.

Meanwhile local shepherds Mr John Dagg and Mr Frank Moscrop realised an aircraft had crashed and, assembling a small search party of locals, set off up the hillside despite the blizzard. With visibility almost zero, their only hope was Sheila, Mr Dagg's sheepdog, which they had brought along with them. It was Sheila who discovered the survivors several hours later with Sergeant Smith feeling her licking his face before summoning her master. Sheila then led the group back down the mountain to Mr Dagg's cottage. They had just reached the cottage when they heard the bombload from the B-17 explode. After a telephone call, transport was arranged to take the airmen to the same sick bay as their crewmates.[156]

The crash attracted press coverage in the home towns of some of the crewmen involved. The *Chicago Tribune*, for example, reported the details of the crash, briefly relating how the bomber crashed onto a mountain peak in a blizzard. The account went on to name the dead crewmen before revealing that amongst the survivors was William R. Kaufman, a native of Chicago (he lived at 2317 North Rockwell Street). The report detailed how a 60-year-old shepherd had led a rescue party of nine men 'in a three hour climb up the steep mountain while the storm raged'.[157]

The surviving crew of the B-17 maintained links with their rescuers and visited on several occasions (the first was to support the unveiling of a memorial consisting of one of the aircraft's propellers; it has since been vandalised and sadly no longer exists) including the 1995 unveiling of the memorial to all aircrew lost in the Cheviots.[158]

Sir William Beveridge became MP for Berwick-upon-Tweed (Public Domain).

The people of Northumberland were wished a merry Christmas by the new MP for Berwick, William Beveridge, who spent the festive period of 1944 at Rothbury. In a letter to local newspapers Beveridge said he was happy to be spending Christmas in Northumberland and wished Christmas greetings to Northumbrians and all those from the county who had left to fight in the war. The letter went on to express the hope that this might be the last wartime Christmas but that if it was not then he was sure the country would still emerge victorious to a better future.[159]

The end of the year saw some changes in the established order in Rothbury when local physician Dr Hedley announced his retirement after working in the village for over forty years; for the last two decades he had been in partnership with Dr Armstrong OBE. Dr Armstrong had only just returned to the village after his release from the Royal Army Medical Corps (RAMC) following five years' service. Dr Hedley was well known throughout Northumberland as he had worked for the county council and held many local medical appointments in the county.

CHAPTER SEVEN

1945

Towards Victory

Despite the success of D-Day the training of young members of the armed forces still took a deadly toll. On 17 January a tragedy occurred on the River Coquet which claimed the lives of ten young trainee soldiers, all aged 18, from 10th Battalion, Duke of Wellington's Regiment and the DLI. The young men were in an assault boat on the river at Guyzance when the boat was swept over the weir and capsized throwing them into the river. As the young men were carrying heavy loads of equipment they could not swim and all ten drowned. At the time of the accident the Coquet was in spate after heavy rain and the officer in charge had ignored warnings from locals and from his sergeant that the river was in far too dangerous a state to mount such an exercise; surviving soldiers were warned not to reveal details of the incident but it was reported locally.[160] Wartime censorship meant that reporting of the incident was

*Private John William Wilson, DLI, one of the ten teenage soldiers to be killed in the tragic accident on the River Coquet (*Evening Chronicle*).*

quickly hushed up and it was not until relatively recently that the full story came to light. One of the men, Private Percy Gibson Clements, had only joined the army in August 1944 and his local newspaper, the *Hartlepool Northern Daily Mail*, was one of the newspapers to report the incident at the time, along with the *Evening Chronicle*.

Rationing was still a focus for debate with anxiety being expressed throughout north Northumberland at plans for the distribution of nuts and oranges. Alnwick Rural District Council heard in January how, despite the government's agreement to allow a quarter of a pound of nuts per ration book, some people were being deprived of their fair ration because of localised population fluctuations. Councillors used the example of the village of Warkworth which before the war had a population of 713 but which had seen an influx of the wives of soldiers during the war years increasing the population beyond 1,000. If every one of these newcomers bought oranges and nuts, they argued, then some people would have to go without. The council agreed to put their concerns to the divisional food office and to await their answer.

In Berwick at the same time there was concern over the town's gas and electricity supply. There had been a power cut on 18 January which had caused some complaints and there were ongoing concerns over the gas supply which for several years had been inadequate. The council met a week later to discuss the gas supply but not everyone was convinced that the townspeople were aiming their complaints at the right people. In a two-hour discussion, which was described by the *Berwick Advertiser* as 'fast and furious', little progress was made. The paper opened its account with the following: 'The gas supply for domestic consumption is said to be short in supply, the same cannot be said for another type of what is called "gas", but which is not of so useful a type.' The newspaper reported that the housewives of the town were complaining to the councillors rather than directly to the company which was responsible for the supply. 'If we do not like the quality of the food we get from shops, do we go to the Councillors and shout about it? We go straight to the shop concerned and give the shopkeeper a bit of our mind, or else to the Food Office ... and ask to be allowed to change our ration book.'[161]

Throughout January the *Berwickshire News* ran articles advising housewives how to make items on their ration books stretch. The advice included such suggestions as mixing sugar with saccharin, saving sugar when making cakes by substituting jam, marmalade or syrup or adding baking powder to sour fruits when cooking. Other advice given in January included removing fat from cooked or uncooked meat and rendering it down for use in the kitchen, and clarifying the fat from stews, soups and the dripping from roasting so that it could be reused. Housewives were also advised to save the wrapping paper from butter, margarine and cooking fat in order to use it for greasing cake tins and for wrapping cheese to prevent it from drying out.

Those on the home front continued to be kept up to date on the fortunes of loved ones who were involved in the fighting. In early March the people of Alnwick were informed that a local man who had recently been at home on leave, Lieutenant W. Avery of Shipley Lane, had been promoted to the rank of Captain. The newly promoted Captain Avery had previously been a Sergeant in the Northumberland County Constabulary and had two brothers who were also serving abroad. One, Robert, had joined the RAF in 1944 but subsequently transferred to the Army and was by March abroad while the third brother, George, had gone ashore with the DLI on D-Day and was still involved in the fighting.

For the Welsh family of Berwick there was sad news when it was revealed that one of their sons, Lance Sergeant Thomas Welsh, 4th KOSB, had died of wounds in hospital in Britain. The son of William and Hannah Welsh, Thomas, or 'Tommer' as he was commonly known, was a former employee of Messrs W.B. Skerry & Sons, butchers, of Marygate. He was a keen cyclist and had been a pre-war member of St. Mary's Church Club. The funeral of Sergeant Welsh took place in his hometown on the final day of February. Soldiers from the Infantry Training Centre acted as pall bearers and the last post was sounded by a bugler. A large number of townsfolk attended along with members of the forces and there were wreaths from his regiment as well as from residents of the street, Crispin Road, in which he lived. William and Hannah must have been concerned as they had a further three sons who were serving: Officer Cadet W. Welsh, Rifle Brigade; Sergeant J. Welsh, Duke of Wellington's Regiment; and Sapper G. Welsh, Royal Engineers.

Many of the men from Northumberland who gave their lives during the war served in the bombing campaign mounted by RAF Bomber Command. Of these brave men, many lost their lives in action against enemy targets, but others lost their lives in the tragic accidents which were part and parcel of wartime flying. Amongst these in 1945 was Sergeant Thomas Aidan Gibson, RAFVR. Sergeant Gibson was a navigator in a Halifax III of 640 Squadron when he and his crew were tasked for a raid on an oil refinery at Wanne-Eickel on 2 February. After taking off from its base at Leconfield the aircraft was observed to either lose or reduce power and bank steeply. This caused the heavily laden bomber to crash into Lakes Wood near Beverley and six of the seven-man crew, including Sergeant Gibson, were killed. Sergeant Gibson was a native of Bamburgh and his mother saw her son buried in the local churchyard. The loss suffered by Mrs Gibson was particularly poignant as her husband had died seventeen months previously; the grieving Mrs Gibson had a joint inscription for both her son and husband placed on the headstone at St. Aidan's.

In addition to the death notices which appeared in local newspapers, many of those grieving families who had lost loved ones in action against the enemy placed *in memoriam* notices in special 'Roll of Honour' sections to their loved ones on the anniversaries of their deaths. In early March a notice appeared commemorating 21-year-old Flying Officer Francis John Nixon of Belford, who had lost his life while piloting Lancaster I (DV294, QR-R) of 61 Squadron in an attack on Augsburg.[162] In the notice his family paid tribute not only to Flying Officer Nixon but also to 'his gallant crew', all six of whom had also been killed.[163]

As it became clearer that an Allied victory in Europe was all but inevitable, some restrictions were relaxed. For the first time since war began a brief weather forecast, forecasting a light frost, was broadcast for the benefit of farmers and gardeners. The blackout, which had been reduced to a 'dim-out' in September 1944, was finally relaxed altogether on 19 April but the many communities along the north Northumberland coast still had to put up with the dim-out as the Admiralty did not want to give submarines off the coast information about their location. Throughout March the people of Berwickshire heard numerous explosions as a large minefield at Pease Bay was removed by the Army.

There were sombre scenes around Northumberland when the news of President Roosevelt's death was announced on 12 April. Flags were flown at half-mast at all public buildings and funeral bells were rung to coincide with the funeral on 17 April.

At the end of April the National Savings Flag was flown from Berwick Town Hall as the authorities declared that the town had successfully raised the total sum of £2,000,000 (over £77,000,000 today). This was a magnificent achievement for a town which had fewer than 7,000 residents (6,725 in 1938) and demonstrates the commitment which communities in north Northumberland had towards supporting the war effort. Taking a population of 7,000 that would mean an average donation of over £11,000 per head; even looking at the municipal borough population of 12,317 this would still mean an average of £6,300 per head.

The signs of a gradual wind-down on the home front came with the standing down of the civil defence forces on 2 May. This meant that all part-time members of the Civil Defence Service, the Observer Corps (though not along the coasts) and the National Fire Service were released from service.

As news of the end of the war in Europe broke around north Northumberland people came out into the streets to celebrate. On 7 May the people of Berwick took to the streets believing a rumour that the Prime Minister was shortly to declare victory in Europe. Although the crowds dispersed when informed that the announcement would instead take place the next day, bunting began to appear and shop windows were decorated with Union Jack flags – scenes repeated across the county. With the news confirmed that Germany had declared an unconditional surrender and the announcement that the following day would be VE-Day, even more flags appeared around the communities of Northumberland and an atmosphere of 'tense excitement' developed.[164]

The next day people once again took to the streets, shops were closed and all members of the forces serving at home were given the day off. Red, white and blue buttonholes and favours were a common sight throughout the day. Rain however 'dampened the ardour of those out to celebrate this victory' and kept most people indoors. People left the streets to listen to the Prime Minister's speech in the afternoon and the town was almost deserted except for a group who gathered outside the Mayor's shop on High Street to listen to the Prime Minister from there. Celebrations were taking place under shelter however and villages, while church bells rang to celebrate the end of the war with Germany.

Many communities organised parties at local venues and impromptu dances, concerts and street parties were held in most towns. In Tweedmouth the people from Kiln Hill, Osborne Road and Mill Strand all had parties. On Tuesday those from Kiln Hill held their party in the Mitchell Memorial Hall while those from Mill Strand held theirs at St. Bartholomew's Church Hall. On Wednesday it was the turn of those from Osborne Road who held their party in the same venue. Bonfires were also popular and drew people outside; these included a large bonfire on the green at Middle Street in Spittal.

The 9th of May was declared a general holiday in most of Northumberland with Sunday timetables on the trains, all businesses being closed and no mail deliveries. A range of festivities took place across the county with, again, a large number in the Berwick area. The weather improved in the afternoon and a concert outside the Town Hall by the band from the Infantry Training Centre attracted a large crowd. After the concert the band marched across the bridge to give another performance at Tweedmouth. On their march they were followed by a large part of the audience, many of whom danced along the route. Tweedmouth Modern School was taken over for the hosting of a fancy dress party for the inhabitants of Farne Road and Sunnyside Crescent.

The improving weather resulted in what was described as 'a lovely May evening, with warm wind and sunshine' and the people of Berwick finally took to the streets en masse to celebrate. The celebrations included street parties and groups of dancers. Large groups danced until the early hours in front of the Mayor's shop, at Blakewell Gardens and, following an open air concert, at Highfields.

Church services were well attended with a voluntary early service at Berwick Parish Church attracting between 300 and 400 service personnel. The evening service was attended by the Mayor, the Sheriff and many members of the town council, as well as by a large number of the public.

More formally, a freedom ceremony was held at Berwick council chamber when a young sub-lieutenant in the Navy, Jack Arthur Gregg, was inducted as a Freeman of the Borough. Not only was Berwick-born Sub-Lieutenant Gregg the first freeman to be appointed following the declaration of peace, he was also the youngest.

As the news sank in, local committees began to act and more formal events were organised. At Berwick, the Berwick-upon-Tweed Welcome Home and Memorial Fund organised a 'Grand Victory Ball' at the Corn Exchange. Music was provided by the band of the King's Own Yorkshire Light Infantry and the committee promised 'Non-Stop Dancing from 9 p.m. to 2 a.m.' Tickets, priced at 5s, were limited and people were urged quickly to purchase them from a number of locations in the town or from members of the committee.

BERWICK-UPON-TWEED WELCOME HOME & MEMORIAL FUND
(Registered under the War Charities Act, 1940).

GRAND VICTORY BALL
—— I N ——
CORN EXCHANGE, BERWICK,
—— O N ——
THURSDAY, MAY 17.
Non-Stop Dancing from 9 p.m. to 2 a.m.
MUSIC BY BAND OF K.O.Y.L.I. (by kind permission of the O.C.).
TICKETS, limited in number (from Fred Stott & Son, Marygate, Shops, and members of the Committee). 5/- Refreshments extra.

Advert for the Victory Ball held at Berwick to celebrate Victory in Europe (Berwick Advertiser).

After the two-day-long celebration of VE-Day the local press sought to remind people that victory must still be won against the Japanese (at a possibly high cost) and that demobilisation could take some time. Furthermore, although the newspapers realised that people on the home front had struggled throughout the war years and were now looking forward to a reduction in restrictions and a return, perhaps, to happier more carefree times, it must be realised that the situation was still bleak and that rationing and such would likely continue for some considerable time. Warning against over-optimism, the newspapers spoke of the need for extensive reconstruction work in the country. The *Berwick Advertiser* stated that immediate action was necessary and cautioned against heeding those who put their own interests in front of those of the town. Of more immediate concern was the need to increase funding for the town's welcome home fund to ensure that its efforts were 'worthy of what the men and women on service have been doing'; a target of £15,000 (about £600,000 today) was set.

On 9 May the Bamburgh sessions took place. Given the circumstances it is not surprising that the magistrates were willing to show an unusual clemency on minor cases such as that of two Chathill farmworkers, Thomas and Elizabeth Scott, who had been accused of riding bicycles without lights in Seahouses. Superintendent Spratt, on behalf of the magistrates, asked for the cases to be dismissed, the charges dropped and any fees remitted. The clerk asked if this was 'a special dispensation of mercy on account of V.E. Day?' and was answered that that was indeed the case.[165]

Over the course of the weeks before and after VE-Day there began the arrival back home of those unfortunates who had been held as prisoners of war in Germany. These men, many of whom had been taken prisoner in 1940, all had tales of hardship to tell and many had been forced to march huge distances across Germany with little or no food during the last weeks of their captivity. Needless to say the returning men were extremely warmly welcomed by their communities. During the VE-Day week a batch of six Northumberland Fusiliers, all of whom had been taken prisoner in 1940, arrived back at Berwick after travelling on the early morning train. Five of the men came from Tweedmouth (Fusiliers T.R. Rae; A. Hay; G. Rutherford; G. Dixon; and J. Reap) while one was a native of Chatton (Fusilier Matthew Laidler). Others to arrive during this time included Private J.S. Aitchison, Queen's Own Cameron Highlanders, who after arriving at the station at Berwick was driven by motorcar to his home at Easington Grange, Belford, where he found a Union Jack flying from the chimney. Another was CSM Smart, Royal Northumberland Fusiliers, who was a pre-war postman in Wooler and who had been one of those former servicemen (he had served during the First World War) who had been responsible for restarting a Territorial company in his hometown before the war. CSM Smart had seen action in France during the Blitzkrieg and had been captured at Dunkirk.

The people of Northumberland were quickly faced, in common with the rest of Britain, with a general election and campaigning began in fierce fashion with many, especially in the forces, seemingly eager to vote for change. Although the election was held on 5 July it was not until close to the end of the month that results were announced. Labour won a resounding victory with many northern seats changing hands. At Berwick the result was announced outside the County Buildings at Haddington in front of a small crowd. The seat (Berwick and Haddington) had previously been held by Captain McEwen (Unionist) with a majority in 1935 of 5,540 but on this occasion the Labour candidate, Councillor J.J. Robertson, won with a majority of 3,157. During the campaign Robertson had become one of Labour's most effective campaigners (or, as the newspapers put it, 'propagandists') in north Northumberland and Scotland. A native of the Shetland Isles, Councillor Robertson had been involved in the Labour movement for over twenty years and had fought at the Battle of Jutland in 1916. His wartime career had been in Scotland as a staff speaker for the Ministry of Information (MoI) and later as Chief Labour Officer (Scotland) for the Home Timber Production Department. Demonstrating the willingness of people to become involved with the campaign, voter turnout was very high at seventy per cent.

However, Labour did not sweep the board and in the Berwick-upon-Tweed constituency the Conservative candidate, Lieutenant Colonel R.A.F. Thorp, won the seat by almost 2,000 votes. This could be partly explained by the fact that there were three candidates for this seat and that Liberal and Labour split the opposing votes. The results were as follows:

Candidate	Party	Vote
Lt-Col. R.A.F. Thorp	Conservative	12,315
Sir William Beveridge	Liberal	10,353
Councillor J. Davis	Labour	5,780

The period between VE-Day and VJ-Day seems to have seen a general slackening of enthusiasm towards the previously well-followed patriotic charitable campaigns. A meeting of Glendale National Savings Committee shortly before the victory over Japan could attract only a small attendance. The meeting was told that efforts to save must continue even after the war and a 'Thanksgiving' campaign was arranged for between 27 October and 3 November with a target of £60,000 (over £2,300,000 today) to be raised in the area.

Conservative candidate Lieutenant Colonel R.A.F. Thorp won the Berwick-upon-Tweed seat by almost 2,000 votes in the General Election (Berwick Advertiser).

Although VE-Day had been met with great joy, the war against the Japanese carried on for many Northumbrians, and for their families the anxiety continued as they awaited word from loved ones fighting far across the globe.

Although it had been clear for some months that Japan would be defeated the fighting to the very end was vicious with many Allied casualties. When VJ-Day was eventually announced on 16 August there was a curious attitude. On the one hand there were 'universal manifestations of rejoicing and deep-seated feelings of relief ... the re-emergence of hopefulness' being shown in a variety of ways.[166] On the other hand, some Northumbrians resented the government instructions on 'how to celebrate a victory' which advised that people could 'celebrate with "bells, bands and bunting"'. The *Berwick Advertiser*, for example, accused the advice of being grandmotherly and of showing a lack of understanding of the situation throughout the country claiming that people could hardly put bunting out when they didn't have any and that shortages meant that there was little material for celebratory bonfire material. While many of the younger generation celebrated raucously the more general prevailing attitude was one of sober satisfaction, relief and reflection. People had sat up to listen to the news broadcast at midnight in expectation of an announcement and as soon as the news came through, rockets and fireworks were fired in many Northumberland communities. At Berwick the Mayor went with his son to waken the town's bell-ringer and his wife, and together the four rang a victory peal at the Town Hall. The sound of the bells brought people onto the streets to celebrate. Amongst the celebrants were women wearing only their night attire and coats, several even still had their hair in curlers! As the party went on music was provided along with a bonfire and further fireworks in front of the Town Hall. Elsewhere in the town the offices of the local newspaper were lit with a large V sign and, despite the concerns expressed above, flags did appear outside many premises.

The party continued until around 4.30 am and later that morning the streets were once again thronged with a prevailing holiday atmosphere. Shops selling flags and fireworks had lengthy queues outside them, as did bakers and grocers as anxious housewives attempted to secure supplies in case of a closure of the shops. The worsening weather in the afternoon failed to dampen spirits with locally-based sailors joining in the festivities in Church Street where a lorry was commandeered. Fireworks were a continual backdrop while local youngsters made a valiant attempt to keep the bonfire in front of Town Hall burning for the evening's celebrations.

In the evening the celebrations continued unabated with huge crowds assembling around the bonfires. When the bonfire in front of the Town Hall ran out of material some young folk ripped up the wooden railings from around the steps to the hall and threw them on too! This particular bonfire was kept going right through the celebrations with locals gleefully adding items to stoke the fire, including old mattresses and 'a weird and wonderful collection'.[167] As well as those celebrating outside, many houses hosted private parties which were either impromptu or had been prearranged for the announcement of final victory. At very short notice a thanksgiving service was also organised at Berwick Parish Church which the Mayor attended along with a very large congregation.

The second day of the VJ-Day celebrations were marred in some parts of Northumberland by incessant and heavy rain but despite this the people of Berwick once more took to the streets, while a dance at the Corn Exchange was very well attended and the town's picture houses saw good trade. In the evening the bonfires were again relit and even more fireworks than the previous day were let off. On both days the Berwick Serviceman's Club was extremely busy. Although the troops had been given the first day off, the rain in the afternoon drove hundreds to take temporary shelter in the club and the second day's downpours once again saw the club extremely busy. The children of the Meadows were largely responsible for organising their own victory party which consisted of tea and games at the tennis pavilion. The event, which was for approximately thirty-five children, was a success largely due to the willingness of the local residents to throw open their homes and provide ingredients for 'a bumper tea'.[168]

The scenes of celebration seen in Berwick were repeated throughout north Northumberland in communities both large and small. In the small village of Branxton, for example, a large bonfire was erected on the green, thanksgiving services were well attended, the entire village was bedecked in flags and a dance in the village hall was a great success. Likewise at Scremerston, the village was festooned with flags, festivities included the parade of the village's brass band through the village to the church where they provided musical accompaniment for the thanksgiving service, and a tea was held for local children in the hall. The almost obligatory victory dance was held in the evening with a large bonfire and fireworks display with musical accompaniment provided by Smallman's Band. On the following day a concert was given in the village hall by the Black Diamonds' Concert Party with patriotic and sentimental songs foremost including *Colonel Bogey*, *There's Something About a Soldier* and *Land of Hope and Glory*. The concert was followed by another dance which again featured Smallman's Band and the hall was 'crowded to its utmost capacity'.[169]

At Tweedmouth the celebrations went on for three days and nights with fireworks, bonfires and dancing. The celebrations seem to have been particularly exuberant in the vicinity of Kiln Hill. Many communities continued to organise more formal celebrations throughout the following week with the residents of Sunnyside Crescent taking part in a victory party at Tweedmouth Modern School. The festivities included a fancy dress competition and parade, races for children in the school yard, a sale of knitted goods which raised £4 for the Welcome Home Fund, and refreshments consisting of tea, lemonade, ice-cream and sweets. Spittal also had a fancy dress parade, led by a number of local women dressed up as John Bull, Kilties, Peace (riding on a pony) and Britannia (riding on a horse and trap). The parade was accompanied by more than 170 children with accompanying adults. After the parade the children were treated to ice-cream and jelly at St. John's School and upon leaving were each presented with a shilling. Fancy dress parades and parties seem to have been a popular VJ-Day activity across Northumberland with many towns and villages holding them. At Longhorsley a fancy dress parade for local children took place with small prizes on offer.

Longhorsley children in fancy dress for VJ-Day (from collection of Bill Ricalton).

On Sunday, 19 August, a large and impressive thanksgiving service took place at Berwick Parish Church. The procession went from the Town Hall to the church and back again and was led by the Mayor and Sheriff. Also foremost in the procession were representatives from Northumberland County Constabulary and Special Constables, the Infantry Training Centre, the Auxiliary Territorial Service (ATS – which consisted of the emergency services, First Aid Nursing Yeomanry, and the Women's Legion), men of the Royal Artillery (based at the Old Barracks), Boys Scouts and Cubs, Girl Guides and Rangers, Air Training Corps (ATC) and representatives of the Council. During the service the vicar, Reverend W.B. Hicks, mentioned the fears that had been felt over the prospect of what 'another "D-Day" on the shores of Japan might mean'.[170] Thankfully, that dreadful prospect had been erased by the Japanese capitulation. Mr Hicks also alluded to the worries of those who had loved ones who were being held prisoner by the Japanese as it was well known that many had been tortured and, indeed, murdered by their captors. Mr Hicks had a particular concern for those serving in Burma as the country had been his home for fourteen years; at the end of the service a collection for the church in the Far East raised the sum of £39.

On VJ-Day the *Berwick Advertiser* had published a special commemorative edition similar to that for VE-Day and the paper was rapidly sold out with many wishing to keep the edition to pass down to future generations. The commemorative edition included photos of men from the area who had been wounded or were being held as PoWs. Amongst the men mentioned by the Reverend Hicks as being prisoners of the Japanese were Sergeant Mark A. Lowrie of Lowick, Regimental Sergeant Major John Mosgrove of Peterfield (*sic*) House, Berwick, Corporal Thomas Ryan, and Fusilier T. Johnston of Palace Green, Berwick. Private R. Virtue was also mentioned as having been wounded in action against the Japanese in Burma.

Demonstrating the confusion over the fate of many men in the Far East theatre of operations, three of those listed as being prisoners had in fact died. One of those mentioned in the paper was Company Sergeant Major John Fraser Wilson, 13th Battalion, The King's Regiment (Liverpool), who was the 29-year-old son of John and Margaret Wilson of Castlegate, Berwick. CSM Wilson had been reported missing while serving in Burma and information was then

Corporal Thomas Ryan, a prisoner of the Japanese (Berwickshire News).

Sergeant Mark A. Lowrie, another prisoner of the Japanese (Berwickshire News).

Regimental Sergeant Major John Mosgrove of Petersfield, Berwick, a captive of the Japanese (Berwickshire News).

received that he was likely to be a prisoner of war. Sadly this later information was untrue and CSM Wilson was later reported to have been killed on 30 April 1943. Another was 22-year-old Fusilier Thomas Henry Ryan, 9th Royal Northumberland Fusiliers. It had been suspected that Thomas had been taken prisoner, along with his brother Corporal Thomas Ryan, during the fall of Singapore but it was later learned that he had lost his life at the end of that battle on 5 February 1942.[171] The third was 27-year-old Fusilier James Phorson Smith, 9th Royal Northumberland Fusiliers. From the tiny hamlet of Mindrum, Fusilier Smith was also reported to be in Japanese

Private R. Virtue, wounded fighting against the Japanese (Berwickshire News).

hands in Malaya but it transpired had died in captivity on 30 June 1943.[172] Fusilier Smith was one of the 93,000 to 113,000 who lost their lives while working on the infamous Burma-Siam railway project.[173] For his parents the news of his death was a heavy blow as they were reported to have been 'looking forward to receiving a cable to inform them that he had been liberated and would be coming home'[174] and James's younger brother Robert had been killed in 1941 as a Sergeant in RAF Bomber Command.

Amongst the many casualties from 9th Battalion, Royal Northumberland Fusiliers, who died while in the captivity of the Japanese was Sergeant Angus Armstrong (41) who died of malaria in Siam. Sergeant Armstrong is something of an enigma as records indicate that his widow lived at Felton and had at one time lived in Morpeth but Sergeant Armstrong is not mentioned on either of the memorials in these locations. Similarly there is some confusion over the date of his death as the CWGC website gives this as 19 July 1945 but a record assembled by the commanding officer of the battalion, Lieutenant Colonel H.S. Flower, records his death as having occurred in 1943 at Sonkrai, Siam.

*CSM John Fraser Wilson, killed in Burma on 30 April 1943 (*Berwickshire News*).*

Throughout September news continued to filter through of the fates of men taken prisoner at Singapore. Captain Henry G. McCreath wrote home to his wife in Berwick to reassure her that he was safe and that two other officers, Captains Archie Veitch and Tom Fairbairn, were safe in the same camp as himself, but McCreath also informed her that several local men had died while in captivity. Amongst the Berwick men were three former Berwick Grammar School students, 22-year-old Fusilier Thomas Purves Johnston, 21-year-old Corporal John Alexander 'Jack' Forster, and 35-year-old Sergeant Ambrose Townsley.[175] At Belford Mr and Mrs Robertson heard the sad news that their only son, 26-year-old Fusilier Robert Robertson, 9th Royal Northumberland Fusiliers, had died in captivity on 4 September 1943.[176]

*Fusilier James Phorson Smith survived the Battle for Singapore only to die in Japanese captivity in 1943 (*Berwickshire News*).*

For other families there was better news. Mrs McGee of Less Lane, Tweedmouth, received the welcome news that her husband, Corporal

Captain Henry G. McCreath wrote home to inform his wife of the fates of prisoners of the Japanese (Berwickshire News).

Captain Archie Veitch, a survivor of several years of Japanese imprisonment and forced labour (Berwickshire News).

Captain Fairbairn, yet another taken prisoner at Singapore (Berwickshire News).

Fusilier Thomas Purves Johnston, died while a prisoner of the Japanese (Berwickshire News).

Corporal John Alexander 'Jack' Forster, died while working on the infamous Burma-Siam railroad (Berwickshire News)

Sergeant Ambrose Townsley, another casualty of the Burma-Siam railroad (Berwickshire News).

William McGee, who had been reported missing in action in Burma in 1943, had been liberated by Allied forces at Rangoon and would shortly be on his way home. Another Tweedmouth man, Driver William MacDonald, wrote to his parents in September informing them that he was safe in India and would be returning home soon.

Many communities had heard nothing from men taken prisoner at Singapore and the end of the war finally brought news. In the small town of Wooler what had been described as 'three and half years of silence' were ended when Private Robert Stewart of the Argyll & Sutherland Highlanders wrote to his mother at Glenavon, Wooler, to say that he was safe in Australia and was looking forward to returning home. The news was warmly welcomed by many of the townsfolk as Robert was a popular member of the community where he was employed as a conductor for the United Bus Company.

Corporal William McGee. Listed as missing in Burma since 1943, he was later found and repatriated (Berwick Advertiser*).*

The tiny village of Glanton received good news about two of its sons who had been prisoners for several years. Fusilier T. Wealleans wrote to his mother to let her know that he had been liberated by Allied troops while Sergeant Kenneth Johnston, who had served in France and been evacuated at Dunkirk, wrote to his parents assuring them that he was safe and well. Sergeant Johnston was well known in north Northumberland as before the war he had been a member of the Coronation Dance Band which had played at a large number of dances across the county since its forming in 1937.

At Norham four local men wrote to reassure parents that they had survived the horrors of captivity by the Japanese. Fusilier Henry Scott, a former groom employed at Rothbury, reported that he was at Bombay and hopeful of a quick return to Britain, while Fusilier J. Shepherd reported that he was in Australia. Fusilier James Virtue, another former bus conductor with United, also cabled his parents to tell that he was safe and had been liberated. The parents of Fusilier Harry Weatherburn would have been overjoyed to receive news that he was also safe and well as he had been reportedly taken prisoner along with his two brothers at Singapore. Sadly one of the Weatherburn brothers, 33-year-old Corporal John Weatherburn, had in fact died on 15 February 1942.[177]

Over the course of the next few days and weeks some of the restrictions of wartime Britain were relaxed or dispensed with. The

Longhorsley Air Raid Wardens in 1945 (from collection of Bill Ricalton).

Longhorsley Home Guard at stand-down in 1945 (from collection of Bill Ricalton).

Longhorsley Red Cross in 1945 (from collection of Bill Ricalton).

Longhorsley Observer Corps (from collection of Bill Ricalton).

petrol ration was increased, sporting events such as weeknight horse and greyhound racing were restored along with the restrictions on football crowds and the keeping of racing pigeons. Cars were no longer required to be immobilised and fireworks, as we have seen, were made available again (although many in the county seem to have pre-empted this with celebrations on VJ-Day anyway). Some restrictions, however, were not to go away so quickly with food rationing lasting until 1954.

Everywhere across north Northumberland people experienced varying emotions including relief, elation and sombre reflection. In towns and villages across north Northumberland men and women who had served on the home front met up for final group photographs and for a last chinwag about their experiences. Even small communities such as Longhorsley had the full gamut of service groups with final assemblies of the local Home Guard, Red Cross, Wardens and Observer Corps all taking place in the weeks following the end of the war. Locals also met to formalise the efforts to welcome home returning service personnel and committees organised dinners and dances to show their appreciation of the sacrifices that had been made.

Longhorsley Welcome Home Committee and Returned Servicemen at the Shoulder of Mutton in 1946 (from collection of Bill Ricalton).

Notes

1 *Alnwick & County Gazette & Guardian*, 1 September 1939, p. 3.

2 *Alnwick & County Gazette & Guardian*, 1 September 1939, p. 4.

3 Sir Hugh went on to give good wartime service, being made joint Under-Secretary of State for Air in July 1941 (a post he served in until the end of May 1945). He became 1st Baron Sherwood in August 1941.

4 The Fairey Seal was a three-seat reconnaissance aircraft used largely by the Fleet Air Arm and was, by 1939, obsolete and being retired from service (only 93 were built in total).

5 The pilot of the aircraft in which Corporal Prudhoe lost his life (Flight Lieutenant Bodman) retired from the RAF in 1948 as a Wing Commander who had been mentioned in dispatches.

6 *Alnwick & County Gazette & Guardian*, 1 September 1939, p. 7.

7 *Alnwick Mercury*, 22 September 1939, p. 7.

8 King's College was at that time part of Durham University but in 1963 became the University of Newcastle upon Tyne (now Newcastle University).

9 For a fuller debate on the duties of the War Ag see Wilt, Alan F., *Food for War. Agriculture and Rearmament in Britain before the Second World War* (Oxford University Press, 2001), pp. 182-222.

10 For an extensive debate on the 'Dig for Victory' campaign from a national perspective see Smith, Daniel, *The Spade as Mighty as the Sword. The Story of World War Two's Dig for Victory Campaign* (Aurum Press, 2011).

11 Wilt, *Food for War*, p. 188.

12 Corporal Thompson has no known grave and is commemorated on the Dunkirk Memorial. On the day he died the Tyneside Scottish were involved in a crucial holding action at Ficheux near Arras. After establishing a blocking position the Tyneside Scottish held off repeated attacks by enemy armour. They held their position for several hours sustaining heavy casualties before withdrawing to Dunkirk where the BEF was being evacuated. Corporal Thompson was one of ninety-one fatalities suffered by the battalion during this action.

13 *Berwick Advertiser*, 28 December 1939, p. 6.

14 *Ibid*.

15 *Ibid*.

16 *Ibid*.

17 Another vessel, the 1,086-ton collier SS *Ferryhill*, which was en route from Blyth to Aberdeen with a cargo of 1,200 tons of coal, was sunk a short distance away on the same day. Owned by Aberdeen firm Hall, Russel & Co Ltd, the

Ferryhill struck a mine laid by *U-22* and sank 1½ miles north of St. Mary's Lighthouse. Of her 13-man crew, 11 were killed, while the first mate and second engineer were rescued by the minesweeping trawler HMS *Young Jacob* (skippered by T. Williamson, RNR) and landed at North Shields where they were treated at Preston Hospital.

18 The *U-19* was retired to the status of a training vessel in May 1940 but reactivated in 1942 for service in foreign waters. She was eventually scuttled in September 1944 off the Turkish coast along with three sister boats.

19 *Morpeth Herald*, 12 January 1940, p. 8.

20 *Berwickshire News & General Advertiser*, 15 May 1945, p. 4.

21 This calculation, like all others in the book, is made using the Bank of England's historic inflation calculator.

22 *Daily Mirror*, 25 March 1940, p. 5.

23 *Ibid*, 27 December 1940, p. 3.

24 *Morpeth Herald*, 23 February 1940, p. 5.

25 The crewmen who died were Able Seaman Harald Forfang, Seaman Halfdan Georg Lauritzen, 2nd Engineer Thorbjorn Julius Nilsen, Seaman John Ricard Stjern and First Mate Andreas Torkelsen; all are commemorated on the Memorial for Seamen in Stavern, Norway. They are buried at Berwick.

26 Mr Simpson had experience of naval emergencies having been twice torpedoed during the First World War (the vessels he served aboard were HMS *Lance* (the destroyer which fired the first British shot of WW1) and HMS *Surprise* (a destroyer launched in 1916 and sunk a year later)).

27 In fact 43 Squadron shot down three aircraft on this day (all Heinkel HEIIIs) with one (shot down near Whitby) being the first German aircraft of the war to crash in England. The victor was Flight Lieutenant Peter W. Townsend. 43 Squadron would move to Wick, Scotland, at the end of February before moving south and taking part in the Dunkirk Evacuation and the Battle of Britain (where it obtained sixty confirmed victories) before re-equipping with Spitfires and becoming, in 1942, part of the Desert Air Force and then taking part in the invasion of Sicily and the fighting in Italy and Southern France.

28 The men who were killed were: 45-year-old Mate Roberts Foster English; Deck Hand James Brown, a 66-year-old married man; and Deck Hand Sydney Lockey, a 35-year-old Amble man. Brown and English were recovered from the wreck and buried at Amble.

29 Chevington Cemetery contains the graves of many RAF men from nearby Acklington but also has seventeen German burials of aircrew shot down during the war.

30 It would appear that Wood was killed later in the war but I have been unable to ascertain his identity with certainty. It is possible that he was Midshipman

James Gregory Wood, RNR, who was killed aged 19 (the newspaper describes him as a youth) in October 1942 while based at HMS *Jackdaw*, a Fleet Air Arm base in Scotland.

31 The monkey, unfortunately, was killed.

32 *Daily Mirror*, 1 March 1940, p. 10.

33 Lieutenant Commander White was subsequently awarded the DSO for his actions. He finished the war as Captain White DSO (and two bars). At the time of his promotion to captain he was the youngest captain in the Royal Navy. Captain White died in 1995.

34 The White brothers made history as one of the very few families to have three members present at the D-Day landings. His brother Jock (Captain A.J.R. White) was also captain of a RN vessel while the older brother, Tony, was present as a Royal Observer Corps spotter.

35 *Berwickshire News & General Advertiser*, 2 July 1940, p. 4.

36 *Morpeth Herald*, 12 January 1940, p. 8.

37 *Berwickshire News & General Advertiser*, 14 May 1940, p. 3.

38 *Berwick Advertiser*, 6 June 1940, p. 3.

39 *Ibid.*

40 Sergeant Borthwick is buried at Crèvecoeur-sur-l'Escaut Communal Cemetery alongside his crewmates Flying Officer Arnold James Stuart and Leading Aircraftman James Horace Gwyn.

41 Sebag-Montefiore, H., *Dunkirk. Fight to the Last Man* (Penguin, 2007), p. 161.

42 *Hartlepool Northern Daily Mail*, 16 July 1940, p. 1.

43 *Berwick Advertiser*, 4 July 1940, p. 4.

44 Lieutenant Colonel Fenwicke-Clennell was part of the well-known Northumbrian gentry family and lived at Ponteland. His nephew was killed with the RAF in 1942.

45 Jack had a successful career as a horseracing trainer after the war (winning the Cesarewitch and the Zetland Gold Cup) but suffered ill-health for the rest of his life. He seldom talked of his wartime experiences and was tragically killed in a car crash on his way to a race meeting at Uttoxeter in 1967 aged 59.

46 John and his brother, Peter, appear to have survived the war.

47 Two years after the end of the war the two families were again together but this time in a far more celebratory setting, the marriage of one of the Hattle brothers, Archie, to a Haggerston woman; one of the Arnott brothers, Thomas, was an usher. The wedding was even more celebratory due to the fact that just days before, the groom had won £400 (equivalent to over £15,000 today) on the football pools! (*Berwick Advertiser*, 13 November 1947, p. 7.)

48 *Berwickshire News & General Advertiser*, 6 August 1940, p. 2.

49 *Berwick Advertiser*, 6 June 1940, p. 3.

50 Leading Seaman David 'Davy' Burgon, RNR, has no known grave and is commemorated on the Lowestoft Naval Memorial. The ship on which he served was one of the famous 'football boats', converted trawlers used for minesweeping and patrol work. Equipped as Asdic trawlers, the ships were widely used to hunt U-Boats. Reports indicated that HMT *Blackburn Rovers* picked up a suspected U-Boat and voluntarily entered a British minefield to pursue it but struck a mine which detonated her depth charges. (The author's grandfather was wartime skipper of the HMT *Derby County* from 1939 to November 1940. He then went on to command the HMT *Kingston Crystal* (until March 1942) and the HMT *Lilac* (July 1944 to mid-1945)).

51 *Berwick Advertiser*, 6 June 1940, p. 3.

52 *The Berwick Advertiser*, 7 November 1940, p. 5.

53 This was far more common than many people believe. Large numbers of women campaigned to let them join the Home Guard as full, combat ready, members and at least one unofficial 'amazons' unit was formed. The War Office refused these demands and such units were quickly disbanded with women being largely, but not wholly, relegated to non-combatant duties. For more on this interesting topic see Summerfield, P. & Peniston-Bird, C., *Contesting Home Defence. Men, Women and the Home Guard in the Second World War* (Manchester University Press, 2007).

54 Both Mr Learmonth and Mr Hay appear to have survived the war.

55 For a very good and readable account of the Home Guard in Scotland see Osborne, B.D., *The People's Army. Home Guard in Scotland, 1940-1944* (Birlinn, 2009).

56 Foot, William, *Beaches, Fields, Streets, and Hills. The Anti-Invasion Landscapes of England, 1940* (English Heritage, 2006), p. 199.

57 *Berwick Advertiser*, 13 June 1940, p. 3.

58 *The Berwick Advertiser*, 18 July 1940, p. 3.

59 *Ibid.*

60 For these stories I am indebted to Mr W.A. Ricalton of Longhorsley [sites.google.com/site/longhorsleylocalhistorysociety/ww2].

61 *Morpeth Herald*, 19 April 1940, p. 7.

62 The bridge was quite rightly listed as it is the only remaining example of a medieval fortified bridge in Northumberland.

63 *Morpeth Herald*, 19 April 1940, p. 7.

64 *Morpeth Herald*, 5 July 1940, p. 4.

65 *Morpeth Herald*, 19 July 1940, p. 2.

66 *Ibid.*

67 Tyrer, Nicola, *They Fought in the Fields. The Women's Land Army: The Story of a Forgotten Victory* (Tempus, 2007), p. 28.

68 For a fuller account of the use of female labour in Northumberland agriculture see Iredale, Dinah, *Bondagers. The History of Women Farmworkers in Northumberland and South-East Scotland* (Glendale Local History Society, 2008).

69 *Berwickshire News & General Advertiser*, 23 April 1940, p. 3.

70 *Berwickshire News*, 7 January 1941, p. 1.

71 Bungay, S, *The Most Dangerous Enemy. A History of the Battle of Britain* (Aurum, 2001), p. 214.

72 AVM Saul did not receive the recognition of his more southerly based counterparts but was in many ways an admirable man. Serving as an observer with 16 Squadron flying BE2s and RE8 reconnaissance aircraft, by the end of 1917 he was commanding 4 Squadron (again RE8s) before undertaking a wide range of command roles in the interwar RAF. Commanding 13 Group in 1940 he not only provided protection to the north of England and Scotland but was also responsible for ensuring that the pilots which he dispatched southwards to 11 group were adequately trained and experienced. This was in stark comparison to his 12 Group counterpart AVM Leigh-Mallory. During the first days of September (the height of the Battle of Britain) the pilots sent south by Saul claimed 43 enemy aircraft for the loss of just two pilots while those sent by Leigh-Mallory claimed just seventeen victories and lost thirteen pilots. After Leigh-Mallory took over at 11 Group, Saul found himself appointed Air Officer Commanding 12 Group and then in 1943 he took over as AOC Air Defences Eastern Mediterranean. After retiring in 1944 Saul became chairman of the United Nations Relief and Rehabilitation Administration's efforts in the Balkans before managing the university book shop at the University of Toronto. Retiring in 1959 he died in 1965, aged 74, after being struck by a car.

73 *Berwickshire News & General Advertiser*, 15 May 1945, p. 4.

74 *Berwickshire News*, 7 January 1941, p.

75 *Morpeth Herald*, 11 April 1941, p. 2.

76 *Morpeth Herald*, 23 May 1941, p. 5.

77 *Morpeth Herald*, 13 June 1941, p. 3.

78 The successful pilots were Sergeants Casey and Prytherch.

79 Mr Grey was the son of the late Berwick poet Thomas Grey (see Craig Armstrong, *Berwick-upon-Tweed in the Great War* (Pen & Sword, 2015), p. 44.

80 *Berwick Advertiser*, 1 May 1941, p. 3.

81 *Morpeth Herald*, 13 June 1941, p. 3.

82 Sergeant Collyer, who was just 19, is buried at Chevington where his headstone has the following verse inscribed upon it: 'All you had hoped for, All you had, you gave, To save mankind – Yourself you scorned to save.'

83 Many of the dead from HMS *Patia* are buried in Tynemouth (Preston Cemetery). Three of the Luftwaffe crew survived and were landed at North Shields where they were taken prisoner.

84 In fact the 202nd Brigade took over the defences in November 1940.

85 The 225th Brigade consisted of the following battalions: 10th King's Own Royal Regiment (Lancashire); 14th King's Regiment (Liverpool) (left February 1941); 9th Border Regiment (left November 1941); 9th South Lancashire Regiment (left May 1941); 12th King's Regiment (Liverpool) (May until November 1941); 15th Durham Light Infantry (November 1941); and 11th King's Regiment (Liverpool) (November). The remaining brigade of the Northumberland County Division, the 216th, consisted of: 12th Royal Scots; 13th Highland Light Infantry; 11th Gordon Highlanders; 15th Argyll & Sutherland Highlanders; 9th (Donside) Gordon Highlanders; 7th Seaforth Highlanders; and 9th (Garrison) Green Howards.

86 *Morpeth Herald*, 11 July 1941, p. 5.

87 Some of the funds were used to provide a roll of honour of the names of fifty of those who served. It was housed in St. Cuthbert's Church.

88 *Berwickshire News & General Advertiser*, 12 August 1941, p. 4.

89 *Berwick Advertiser*, 14 August 1941, p. 5.

90 Mr Young had served in WW1 with the Black Watch (Canadian) and had been blinded at Vimy Ridge.

91 By 15 June 1941 Kampfgeschwader 26 had claimed one cruiser, one destroyer, 21 smaller ships and 436,186 tons of merchant shipping.

92 *Berwick Advertiser*, 10 April 1941, p. 5.

93 *Morpeth Herald*, 21 November 1941, p. 2.

94 HMS *Fleur-de-Lys* was launched on the Tees as *La Dieppoise* and was bound for the French navy before the war when she was taken over by the Royal Navy and renamed.

95 *Morpeth Herald*, 5 December 1941, p. 4.

96 *Berwickshire News & General Advertiser*, 17 February 1942, p. 4.

97 *Berwick Advertiser*, 19 February 1942, p. 4.

98 *Berwick Advertiser*, 15 January 1942, p. 5.

99 *Berwick Advertiser*, 7 May 1942, p. 4.

100 *Berwick Advertiser*, 15 January 1942, p. 5.

101 We shall meet Sheila and Mr Dagg later in 1944.

102 The crew reflected Bomber Command's international blend: (Pilot) Sergeant Laurence Warren Hunt (20), RNZAF (died of injuries); (2nd Pilot) Pilot Officer Bertram A. MacDonald, RCAF; (Observer) Sergeant Thomas Walter Irving (23), RNZAF (killed in crash); (Wireless Operator/Air Gunner) Sergeant Frederick George Maple (33), RAF (died of injuries); (Wireless Operator/Air Gunner) Sergeant William H. Allworth, RAF; (Air Gunner) Cyril

F. Glover, RAF. Sergeants Irving, Maple and Hunt are buried at Chevington Cemetery.

103 At this period of the war the chances of a crew surviving a first operational tour of thirty missions was very slim (after completing the tour the aircrew were posted away to train others but could be recalled or volunteer after six months for a second tour of 20 operations. The Pathfinders of 8 Group flew a first tour of 45 operations with a further 15 constituting a second tour. After completing a second tour the aircrew could not be recalled for bomber operations).

104 Sergeant Hall has no known grave and is commemorated on the Runnymede Memorial. He shares this honour with five other members of the crew while the body of his pilot was found near Terningen Lighthouse and buried at Stavne cemetery.

105 The two men killed were Fusiliers George Errington (33) and John Henry Ryan (22); both were buried at sea and are commemorated on the Singapore Memorial.

106 *Berwick Advertiser*, 30 September 1943, p. 6.

107 Happily all seven Fairnington brothers seem to have survived the war.

108 George Scott is buried at Thanbyuzayat cemetery in Myanmar while Charles is buried at Kanchanaburi cemetery in Thailand.

109 All six of this seemingly happy band would appear to have survived the war and returned home safely.

110 Topham went on to become one of the RAF's most successful night fighter pilots of the war with a score of twelve aircraft destroyed, 1 probably destroyed and a further one damaged. He finished the war as a Wing Commander with the DSO, DFC (and bar) and retired in the late 1960s as an Air Commodore.

111 *Morpeth Herald*, 4 December 1942, p. 6.

112 Readers will remember the fate of Edward's uncle Lieutenant Colonel G.E. Fenwicke-Clennell who was taken prisoner in the surrender of 51st Division in 1940. The family had also suffered losses during the First World War when two family members were killed. Captain Thomas Percival Edward Fenwicke-Clennell was killed serving with the Borders & Lothian Horse in Greece in February 1918, and Lieutenant Oswald Fenwicke-Clennell Carr-Ellison was killed in 1915 while serving with the Northumberland Fusiliers as discussed in the author's book *Alnwick in the Great War* (Pen & Sword, 2016).

113 From the crew of seven only the flight engineer Sergeant P.M. Slater survived to be taken prisoner. Those killed, aside from P/O Fenwicke-Clennell were: Flight Sergeant J.P. Warren (navigator); Sergeant R.G. Clarkson, RCAF (bomb aimer); P/O J.A.W. Moffatt DFC (wireless operator); Sergeant J.F. Edwards, RCAF (mid-upper air gunner); and Sergeant J.H. Baker (rear

gunner). The raid in which the crew lost their lives was later adjudged a failure with most bombs falling in open country after the bombers were attracted by a decoy site.

114 Interestingly the six crew members from P/O Fenwicke-Clennell's aircraft are six of only ten British airmen to remain buried in a German civil churchyard; the rest are in Commonwealth War Cemeteries.

115 *Morpeth Herald*, 8 January 1943, p. 5.

116 R. Elliott was based at the Grey Bull garage in the Market Place.

117 *Morpeth Herald*, 17 September 1943, p. 1.

118 *Newcastle Journal*, 7 October 1943, p. 4.

119 *Morpeth Herald*, 5 November 1943, p. 2.

120 Leek Pudding: 8 oz flour; 1 oz fat; 1 oz grated raw potato; two level teaspoons of baking powder; one level teaspoon of salt; 8 oz finely chopped leek; water to mix. Mix together all ingredients and add enough water to create a stiff batter. Place into a greased basin and steam for 1-1½ hours. Serve with gravy or cheese sauce.

121 Vegetable Hot-Pot: 2 oz leeks or onions; 4 oz carrots; 4 oz turnips; ¾ lb potatoes; ½ teaspoon of mixed herbs; ½ teaspoon of salt and pepper to taste. Dice carrots and turnips, slice onions and potatoes. Place carrots, turnips and onions in a dish and cover with water before placing the sliced potatoes on top. Cook for two hours in a moderate oven with a lid on the dish. When peas were in season they could be used instead of one vegetable.

122 Spring Victory: four level teaspoons of dried egg; one carrot; one turnip; 2 oz swede; 2 oz cabbage; two spring onions. For the white sauce: 2 oz margarine; 2 oz flour; ½ oz milk powder; ¼ pint water. Dice and cook vegetables in salted water before draining well. Make the sauce, add vegetables and half the reconstituted egg, mix well and turn onto a tray to cool. Mould into shapes, roll in flour or breadcrumbs and fry until golden brown. Scramble the remaining egg and pile into the middle of the dish before arranging the croquettes around.

123 Corned Beef Pie: three rations of corned beef (6d worth); one cup of finely shredded raw vegetable (carrot, potato, leek swede, etc); one dessertspoon of flour; one Oxo cube; a small piece of fat; shortcrust pastry (made with 6 oz flour and 3 oz fat); one teaspoon of chopped parsley. Melt fat in a small frying pan and fry the vegetable lightly before stirring in the flour and cooking for a few minutes. Add one cup of cold water into which the Oxo cube has been crumbled and stir until thickened. Take off the heat and add cubed corned beef, parsley and salt and pepper to taste. Line a small plate with the pastry and spread on the meat mixture before covering with pastry, crimping edges and decorating with small pastry leaves. Bake in a moderate oven for half an hour.

124 Corned Beef Turnover: 8 oz corned beef; 1½ lbs of potatoes; a small piece of fat; a small onion or, if not available, a teaspoon of chopped parsley; an Oxo cube. Dissolve the Oxo in a small cup of hot water, peel the potatoes and cut them into ½ inch dice. Then dice the meat, mince the onion and mix with the potatoes before seasoning and moistening with the Oxo cube. Melt the fat in a heavy based frying pan until smoking hot and then add the meat and vegetable mixture, flattening it down to form a flat cake. Cover and reduce the heat to a gentle heat and cook for approximately 40 minutes (the potatoes should be cooked and the underside crisp and browned). Fold over and place on a warmed serving plate; garnish with parsley.

125 *Berwick Advertiser*, 29 April 1943, p. 6.

126 *Berwick Advertiser*, 5 August 1943, p. 2.

127 *Berwick Advertiser*, 2 September 1943, p. 4.

128 *Berwick Advertiser*, 23 December 1943, p. 6.

129 For an account of this incident see Wylie, N, *Barbed Wire Diplomacy: Britain, Germany, and the Politics of Prisoners of War 1939-1945* (Oxford University Press, 2010).

130 *Berwick Advertiser*, 29 April 1943, p. 6.

131 Gillam ended the war as an acting group captain with two further bars to his DSO after leading more than eighty sorties against numerous enemy targets following D-Day.

132 Of the men killed in January and February, Flight Sergeant Maynard, Sergeant Dixon and Sergeant Hobbs are buried at Kirknewton, Flight Lieutenant Van-Schaik is buried at Littleover (St. Peter) Churchyard and Sergeant Gleadall at Doncaster Cemetery.

133 On the night in question, three Stirlings assigned to minelaying tasks were lost; the losses were from 75, 90 and 199 Squadrons. Of the twenty-one airmen involved Sergeant Hook was the only survivor. A Halifax of 466 Squadron also crash-landed, without injury to its crew, upon return from a minelaying sortie.

134 The crew who were killed were: (Pilot) Warrant Officer George J.S. Kerr (22), RAFVR; (Navigator) Sergeant Donal F. Wort, RAFVR; (Flight Engineer) Sergent Leonard G. Copsey (20), RAFVR; (Bomb Aimer) Sergeant Ronald Smith (20), RAFVR; (Wireless Operator/Air Gunner) Flight Sergeant Derek A. Holt, RAFVR; and (Air Gunner) Sergeant George W.T. Lucas (22), RAFVR. Warrant Officer Kerr is buried at Chevington Cemetery.

135 Despite suffering burns Sergeant Hook was flying again within two months and by the end of the war was one of the most experienced air gunners in the command having completed more than seventy-five operations. He remained in the RAF after the war and retired as a flight lieutenant in 1977.

136 *The Times*, 3 December, 1943.

137 Flying Officer Bell is commemorated on the Runnymede Memorial.
138 The dead were: (Pilot) Flight Sergeant Robert Fiddes (22), RAFVR; (Flight Engineer) Sergeant Henry Richard Kitchener, RAFVR; (Navigator) Sergeant Robert Brackenridge Hoynes (25), RAFVR; (Air Bomber) Sergeant Kenneth James Dunger (23), RAFVR; and (Wireless Operator/Air Gunner) Sergeant David Williams (29), RAFVR. The surviving members of the crew were Sergeants A.E. Adams and A. Currie.
139 *Daily Mirror*, 17 March 1944, p. 8.
140 *Morpeth Herald*, 5 May 1944, p. 5.
141 *Morpeth Herald*, 24 March 1944, p. 6.
142 *Morpeth Herald*, 2 June 1944, p. 8.
143 The aircraft's eight-man crew were all killed. Pilot Officer Mabon was the only British member in this otherwise Canadian crew (Canadian crews often flew with British flight engineers) and he is buried at Canada Cemetery, Tilloy-lez-Cambrai, where there is also a memorial to the crew.
144 Sergeant Johnston found himself in Stalag Luft 1. He survived the war and was one of four former PoWs who returned to Berwick on the evening of 16 May 1945. The rest of Sergeant Johnston's crew were: Flight Lieutenant E.W. Everritt (Pilot); Sergeant K.H. Jones (Flight Engineer); Sergeant J.R. Stewart (Navigator); Flying Officer J.K.M. Green (Air Bomber); Sergeant J.R. Graham (Mid Upper Gunner); and Pilot Officer A.P. Sinden (Rear Gunner).
145 Flight Lieutenant Bell has no known grave and is commemorated, like his brother, on the Runnymede Memorial. Oddly, neither brother appears to be commemorated in Berwick.
146 Flight Lieutenant Brewis is one of just four Commonwealth casualties buried at Hoorn (all are airmen). Alongside him is his pilot, Flight Lieutenant Arthur Whitten-Brown. Whitten-Brown was the son of Colonel Sir Arthur Whitten-Brown who had been the navigator to John Alcock when the pair had flown the first successful non-stop flight across the Atlantic in 1919.
147 There are 652 Commonwealth burials from the Second World War here and also one Polish burial. There are also 335 German graves in the cemetery.
148 There is some confusion over the date of death. The CWGC lists it as 30 August while most other sources list it as 30 July on the first day of Operation Bluecoat. Most memorials list the date as 30 July so this is the date I have used here.
149 The grave is known as the Livry (Le Repas) Isolated Grave.
150 The crewmen to be killed were: 30-year-old Pilot Officer Herbert Gordon Haddrell (pilot), RAFVR; 21-year-old Sergeant John Neilsen (flight engineer), RAFVR; 22-year-old Warrant Officer Maurice Frederick James (air gunner), RAFVR; and 21-year-old Warrant Officer Geoffrey Symonds (air gunner),

RAFVR. The survivors were: Sergeant John Mahoney (navigator); Sergeant Reid (wireless operator); and Sergeant Hammond (air gunner).

151 The crash site is not easy to reach now but there is still quite a large amount of wreckage visible; the engines were dug out of the peat and removed, and a memorial cross has been erected. Sources report that the Halifax hit a large rock in the peat and disintegrated on impact.

152 Joe himself was left furious after the crew of a Mosquito put in a joint claim for this flying bomb despite the fact that they had opened fire when hopelessly out of range.

153 At first buried at Scheemda as an unknown British airman, Joe's remains were recognised in 1956 and a permanent CWGC headstone was erected; Squadron Leader Joseph Berry DFC (two bars), RAFVR, was 24 when he lost his life. Much of his story comes from the website: hawkertempest.se/ index.php/contributions/stories/117-joe-berry-the-forgotten-ace. Joe's award of two bars to his DFC was very rare with only forty-two similar occurrences during the war. In 1999 Joe's widow Joyce unveiled a memorial plaque to him. In 2015 Joe's medals and mementoes were sold for £17,500 at Anderson & Garland on behalf of his great nephew who lives in Rothbury.

154 *Berwick Advertiser*, 16 November 1944, p. 7.

155 The decline in the Luftwaffe was shown by the fact that from June 1944 B-17 crews were reduced from ten to nine men with one of the two waist gunners being declared surplus to requirement. From late February the remaining waist gunner was also removed although some crews continued to use one or even two regularly or on an ad hoc basis.

156 Keen eyed readers will recognise this as the second rescue that Mr Dagg and Sheila had taken part in. In June 1945 both Mr Dagg and Mr Moscrop were awarded the British Empire Medal for their part in the rescue (this was Mr Dagg's second medal for rescuing downed airmen). Sheila became the first civilian dog to be awarded with the Dickin Medal for animal heroism. In 1946 the mother of Sergeant Turner wrote to Mr Dagg to thank him for his efforts on that day and asked if it might be possible to purchase one of Sheila's puppies. This happened in 1946 when Tibbie, Sheila's first puppy, was sent to Mrs Turner in South Carolina; Tibbie lived for the next eleven years as the town pet of Columbia, South Carolina.

157 *Chicago Tribune*, 26 January 1945, p. 5.

158 Flying Officer Holcombe and Sergeant Turner were buried at the American Cemetery in Cambridgeshire. The survivors all went on to survive the war. Second Lieutenant Kyle was invalided back to the USA in April 1945, Flying Officer Hardy went on to fly a tour of thirty missions before going back to the USA, Sergeants Schieferstein, Kaufmann and Delaney returned to flying and completed another ten or eleven missions, Sergeant Smith

collapsed while on leave and was diagnosed with spinal meningitis; he was declared dead at his base but while in the morgue a US Army doctor noticed he was from the same town in Kentucky and decided to check once more for a pulse; finding a very weak heartbeat he successfully revived Sergeant Smith. The two who attended the 1996 unveiling were George Kyle and Joel Berly.

159 William Beveridge, later 1st Baron Beveridge of Tuggal, was the author of the 1942 report *Social Insurance and Allied Services* (otherwise known as the *Beveridge Report*) and the 1944 report *Full Employment in a Free Society*. These reports formed the basis for the post-war welfare state. Beveridge died at his Northumberland home and is buried at Thockrington Churchyard, north of Hexham.

160 A local woman, Mrs Vera Vagg, researched the incident and was involved in the erection of a memorial to the men in 1995. The dead men were all privates bar one: Percy Gibson Clements (DLI); Lance Corporal Mark Fredlieb (DWR); Alexander Leighton (DLI); John William Wilson (DLI); Ronald Herbert Winteringham (DLI); Kenneth Lee (DLI); Edwin King (DLI); Maurice Masterman Peddelty (DLI); Harold Yates (DLI); and Norman Ashton (DWR).

161 *Berwick Advertiser*, 25 January 1945, p. 8.

162 Flying Officer Nixon is buried along with his crew at Liesse Communal Cemetery.

163 The other crewmen in this all RAFVR crew were: Flight Sergeant James William Devenish (navigator); Flight Sergeant Arthur Thomas Garrett (air bomber); Sergeant William Craig (flight engineer); Sergeant joseph Ernest Chapman (wireless operator); Sergeant Herbert Frederick Bore (air gunner); and Sergeant Henry William John Pain (air gunner).

164 *Berwickshire News Victory Souvenir Issue*, 15 May 1945, p. 5.

165 *Berwick Advertiser*, 10 May 1945, p. 3.

166 *Berwickshire News, VJ-Day Souvenir Issue,* 21 August 1945, p 3.

167 *Berwick Advertiser*, 23 August 1945, p. 6.

168 *Ibid*.

169 *Berwick Advertiser*, 23 August 1945, p. 6.

170 *Berwick Advertiser*, 23 August 1945, p. 6.

171 Both men have no known grave with CSM Wilson commemorated on the Rangoon Memorial and Fusilier Ryan on the Singapore Memorial.

172 Fusilier Smith is buried at Kanchanaburi War Cemetery.

173 Of these victims 13,000 were PoWs (British, Commonwealth, Dutch and American) while a further 80,000-100,000 civilians were killed (mainly forced labour brought from Malaya and the Dutch East Indies or conscripted from Burma or Siam).

174 *Berwickshire News & General Advertiser*, 18 September 1945, p. 4.

175 Fusilier Johnston (who died on 18 July 1943) is buried at Chungkai War Cemetery (Thailand), Corporal Forster (who died on 7 September 1943) and Sergeant Townsley (who died on 26 June 1944) at Kanchanaburi War Cemetery (Thailand).

176 Fusilier Robertson is buried at Kanchanaburi War Cemetery.

177 Corporal Weatherburn is commemorated on the Singapore Memorial.

Index